Her ULTIMATE Pleasure

David DeCitore

Copyright © 2008, 2020 Released October 2020 by David DeCitore

All rights reserved. No part of this publication may be reproduced in any manner, stored in a retrieval system, or transmitted in any form or by any means, electronic, mechanical, photocopying, recording, or otherwise, without the prior written permission of the publisher.

Published by: EroticFlow.com | ISBN 978-0-9832755-7-2

Cover Image has a Premium Commercial License from Shutterstock.com | Background resources from SkinIt.com and DecalSkin.com.

Display of content on mobile devices. Depending on the size of your screen, if you use a large font size, the headings will appear with hyphens.

IMPORTANT: The underlined content represents online research sources and products supplied in the ebook. Links, color charts, and product images are on a webpage URL provided in the Recources section.

Her Ultimate Pleasure
Table of Contents

Testimonials viii

Dedication x

Erotic Flow xi

Content Insights xii

Chapter One - Introduction

The Unique Value and Erotic Pleasures This Book Will Give You and Your Lover

    1.1 The What and The How - The pleasure promise and how this book will deliver it 1

    1.2 Why - The unmet need to provide a detailed step-by-step system to pleasurable anal pleasure . 2

    1.3 For Whom - Erotic delight for women and couples . . 4

    1.4 The Solution and The Benefits - All the HOT rewards you will experience 4

    1.5 The Difference - The pleasurable difference a couple will feel using the techniques in this book . . 5

    1.6 The Results Are In - Research shows women have more and stronger orgasms from anal sex 7

    Chapter Summary 33

Chapter Two - Arouse Her Mind, Body, and Soul
The SEPOR Method and The 7 Nights to Ecstasy

    2.1 Satisfy Her Soul - So you can discover new pleasures with trust 38

    2.2 Seduce Her Body - So her mind eagerly wants more ~ The SEPOR Method 40

    2.3 Communication - Arousing her sexuality to new exciting heights 42

    2.4 The 7 Nights to Ecstasy System - Overview 43

    2.5 Assess How She Feels About Anal Play - So you can design the process exactly for her. . . 45

    2.6 Seduction Philosophy 51

    2.7 Patience is Pleasure 51

    2.8 Set-up Ahead of Time to Be Smooth During 52

Chapter Summary. 53

Chapter Three - 7 Nights to Ecstasy
The Process of Pleasuring Her and Giving Her Thrilling Orgasms Every Step of the Way to Anal Ecstasy

    3.1 The Process In Detail - How to perform every touch, lick, and caress 58

    3.2 Night 1 - Beginning a new world of pleasure 59

        a. Finger Rolls

        b. Palm and Gem Pleasure

    3.3 Night 2 - Feel the warmth of my passion 62
        a. Grooves For Her

3.4 Night 3 - Triple her pleasure 70
    a. Her Pleasure Anatomy
    b. Grooves For Her Pump
    c. Palm and Curve Pleasure

3.5 Night 4 - Vibrate her soul 80
    a. Importance of CT
    b. The oooh OOOHs Technique

3.6 Night 5 - Expand her ecstasy. 84
    a. Pleasure Twists

3.7 Night 6 - Entering the gem of intimacy 89
    a. Grooves For Her
    b. Leave-in
    c. Gem Slides
    d. Waves of Lubrication
    e. My Vibe
    f. The Ass Jiggle
    g. The 5 Steps to Entering Her Gem

3.8 Night 7 - Hear those magical words you've been waiting for, "Give me more, more!. 103
    a. Ride The Grooves

Chapter Summary. 109

Chapter Four - Preparing for Anal Play

Making Anal Play Good, Clean, Fun

4.1 Hygiene - Making the pleasure zones delicious and safe for ultimate delight 116

4.2 Clean Up for Anal Play. 119

4.3 Other Hygiene and Health Considerations 121

4.4 Toys For Explosive Anal Orgasms - Making the process completely pleasurable ... 123

4-5 Lubricants - Enabling wetness to take her to new worlds of pleasure........................ 133

Chapter Summary.................................... 140

Chapter Five - Erotic Anal Play

Delicious Stimulation for Both of You

5.1 Erotic AZ Play and Advanced Positions.......... 144
    a. The E3................................... 145
    b. Palms of Pleasure 147
    c. The V-Spot Massage 148
    d. The V-Spot Massage and Vibe Combo 150
    e. Missionary Work... It's All About Giving 151
    f. Tongue Tingle 152
    g. Pleasure Twists.......................... 153
    h. The CrissCross 154
    i. The Straddle and Flip 155
    j. Good Vibes 158
    k. Pearls................................... 159
    l. Fingertips 160
    m. Eyes Wide Shut 161
    n. Upside Down Gem Spot 164
    o. Gem 69 166
    p. Upside Down V-Lick 167
    q. Ride-Em................................ 168
    r. Ride-Him On All Fours..................... 170
    s. G&G.................................... 171
    t. Reverse Cowgirl Massage.................. 173
    u. Bend Over, Beautiful 174

- v. Naughty Butterfly 176
- w. U-Spot Love 176
- x. Bottoms Up 177
- y. Body Quake 179
- z. Hand Quake 180

5.2 The Spice of Variety 180

5.3 Tips to Maintain Enjoyment -
Consistently enhance the experience 181

5.4 Ever-Evolving Pleasure 184

5.5 Erotic Flow Books 185

Chapter Summary 186

Author Bio 190

Resources 193

Testimonials

Ouch!!! That was what I associated with "anal sex." I had only experienced pain and discomfort when it came to anal sex in my 10 years of sexual history. It had been my experience that every male I encountered had the one fantasy of anal sex and had no clue what it entailed. Anal sex had been introduced to me by several partners and had left me running for the door. I never in my life believed that I could receive any pleasure from it. I simply wanted to do it to please my partner.

I researched how to go about it in a painless manner since it's displayed as pleasurable and painless in porn, but what I found didn't inspire comfort. It wasn't until my boyfriend implemented the techniques in this book and took his time to introduce me to anal sex in a sensual way through this methodical process that I not only was comfortable with anal sex but found it pleasurable. After my first full penetration session, there was no turning back. I wanted to replay the intense orgasm that I had received through anal sex over and over. The methods and process in this book will change your sexual experience when it comes to becoming aroused by anal sex and obtaining an orgasm. It will give you an out-of-body, intimate experience with your partner that I guarantee you have never experienced

—Jennifer M.

When I first tried anal a long time ago with a boyfriend, it was SO painful, and I swore I would never try it again. But then I read this book with my boyfriend, and we tried it, and it was amazing! We went really gradually at first, just like the book suggests, and it didn't hurt. Instead, it felt really good. And over time, I wanted that more than regular sex because it felt so good. I think one thing I didn't understand about anal was that you can still have face-to-face sex, so it can still be intimate and incredibly sexy at the same time.

And doing anal this way, it was easy to stimulate my clitoris at the same time, either by him or with a toy, an incredible combination. I can't say enough about how grateful I am that we learned this technique for anal, and now it's part of our regular sexual repertoire. Oh yeah, and my boyfriend is pretty incredibly happy with it, too. A huge thank you from him!

—Lisa T.

The techniques taught in this book are unlike anything that I have ever read before, and it works! I had tried anal sex before, and it hurt going in, coming out, and during the entire ordeal. I thought it was simply that I didn't like anal sex, but after understanding that there was a correct method, it completely transformed my sex life. After studying these techniques there was absolutely no discomfort in the beginning, which was surprising because he is more endowed than any previous partner I've had. The first time my boyfriend tried it, no pain at all, only pleasure.

Once it was inside, along with some other playful techniques mentioned in the book, I was able to have the most intense orgasm of my life ... and that is not an exaggeration. What I enjoy most about this method is that it doesn't require a big change in my sex life; it complements what I am already doing, with great, easy suggestions. Having this book has added an amazing layer of sensuality that I wasn't aware of. My boyfriend loves it, and I am grateful for it.

—Cynthia G.

Ladies, in an effort to expand the variety in our bedroom, my boyfriend and I read this book. My man has always longed to add anal pleasure to our sex lives, but due to a painful experience in my past, I wrote off anal sex, and judged that it was not for me. We implemented the highly pleasurable and easy techniques, and in time I was experiencing mind-blowing orgasms from clitoral and vaginal stimulation and anal penetration simultaneously!!! My boyfriend is well endowed, and I was skeptical in the beginning, fearing that it might hurt, but it did not. Your man will learn just how to get you relaxed, excited, and eager for this erotic treat!!

—Mariana L.

Dedication

This book is dedicated to the beauty of women and their ultimate sexual ecstasy, to men and the fulfillment they will enjoy from this exciting sexual experience, and to couples and the hot sex and deep connection they will love.

Sign-up for the email list to **get a bonus** pleasuring technique and a sex fantasy with setup, execution, and positions from my new book. You won't be bombarded with emails. I will let you know when my next product is available and if there is an update to this book. Send an email with the subject LIST to info@EroticFlow.com.

Erotic Flow

EroticFlow.com (EF), was started to inspire lovers to seduce each other's mind, body, and soul. EF helps couples cultivate the art of sensual, passionate, and erotic experiences. The aim is to encourage couples to fall in love with pleasuring each other and igniting their sexual hunger.

"Erotic" refers to sensuous and creative sexual expression. "Flow" is when two people connect deeply, savoring each other's energy, and get lost in the moment. It is seducing all the senses to revel in ecstasy. Hence, Erotic Flow means creatively expressing your erotic soul so that your and your lover's energy become one.

Learn more about EF products in the Resources section of this book.

Content Insights

Over the last decade, thousands of women have read this content and provided feedback. Additionally, I have conducted interviews over the last 25 years. Both the feedback and interviews ensure womens' perspectives have been incorporated into the instructions. Ten female editors read the book for content and structure and gave it their blessing. Therefore, along with the female customers that have gone through the system, the guidance about introducing anal sexuality has been vetted from a woman's perspective.

The content has benefited thousands of couples across 12 countries. The feedback they provided is included.

Share The Love Promo: If the research is informative and/or you think the content can help couples have a better anal stimulation and introduction experience, share the book with a friend. I will gift them the ebook. Send a screenshot of purchase to info@EroticFlow.com.

Reviews are the lifeblood for an author to make a difference and enable others learn about a subject. YOUR REVIEW IS GREATLY APPRECIATED. Without it, the years of effort won't be able to help others.

If you already purchased the book, start at Section 1.6, the research and scientific data. Dive into the topics that spark your interest, and to skip to the how-to instructions quickly, start at the Conclusion content of Section 1.6. Instructional images start in Chapter Three. It's essential that you don't risk giving your partner a poor experience by merely scanning the images and content. Invest the time to read the pleasuring process in detail, and you'll both love anal sexuality and have explosive orgasms from it.

Advanced Content

If you bought the book for the advanced techniques, read the Conclusion of Section 1.6, scan the Chapter Two summary, read through Chapter Three, and look for the techniques in bold and the context around them. The activities at the beginning of the process, might be things you're already doing. Review the chapter to see if they are and how the activities can be modified to complement what you already do. Look for the Grooves For Her, Grooves For Her Pump, Palm and Curve Pleasure, Gem Slides, My Vibe, Pleasure Twists, and Ride The Grooves techniques. Read Her Pleasure Anatomy in Night Three. Check out Chapter Four to see if there are differences in your hygiene practice, along with my recommendations for toys and lubes. Chapter Five is where you will find the core of the advanced activities. Focus on hand actions, finger stimulation, and licking details combined with positions and the use of toys to enhance arousal.

Q & A

Isn't this information online for free?

I developed the system over the last 30 years, and after creating the content, I researched many resources to make sure it was unique and not available elsewhere. I studied over 50 books, 237 web articles, 110 YouTube videos, 10 DVDs, and attended four sex conferences with in-person classes on the topic. I spent years researching for you. This book was not pieced together from disparate content in the resources above or from interviews. The system was developed during my relationships and fine-tuned through feedback in the moment of experience.

I invite you to read the book and then review other resources to see if you find a comparable system with as many instructional images published before my copyright dates. If you do, I will gladly refund you for this book and give you my new book as a gift. If the information online effectively enabled pleasurable and painless anal sex, you would not still have lots of lousy experience stories. The Internet has been around long enough for a good strategy to make its way into the overall sexual consciousness, but it has not. Therefore, I poured my heart and soul into developing a caring solution that works and helps couples enjoy deeper intimacy and a new sexual delight.

What are the author's credentials and credibility to write on this topic?

I have a double major in Finance and Marketing with a minor in Psychology, concentration in interpersonal relations and accelerated learning. As well as a Master's degree in Business with course work in statistics and research. I am not a full-time writer. I have a different career than sex. How does that qualify me to write about a solution to introduce anal sex and enhance sexual pleasure? Valid question. First, it starts with compassion. I was injured before and was in significant pain for years. I had to have hundreds of injections because the pills weren't strong enough to help. Pain is invisible, and therefore hard to relate to unless you have experienced it yourself. I found a solution, and the experience made me very compassionate to others who deal with pain.

Many women are subject to an unpleasant experience when attempting to have anal sex due to a flawed process. I knew if I wrote down my solution, I could help women avoid an uncomfortable experience. Moreover, enable couples to discover a new delight and a deeper connection instead of getting frustrated or upset from failed attempts.

Does someone need a degree stamp to develop an effective solution? I believe not. The number of books, articles, educational videos, and classes I have researched over 30 years easily surpasses my master's degree in course work and time invested. Besides, you can study all the content out there and conduct many interviews; if you do not implement the solution across different relationships, you won't have a vetted system. The women from my relationships have encouraged getting the content out to help others. With their support, when I introduced the first version of my content, it reached a Best Sellers rank of #3 in the Psychology of Sexuality, a sales rank in the low 4,000s out of all Amazon books, and was #1 on the topic of anal sex on Amazon (screen-captures are on my Amazon Author's Page).

In addition to the above, I authored the book because creating new sexual experiences is a core passion. My story starts many moons ago... (continued in the Author Bio).

How can a man write a book about the best method to introduce anal sexuality to woman?

This is a frequently asked question because some people say it's not the man having the experience of possible discomfort or embarrassment. I'll explain my experience in developing a solution to this topic.

Although I developed the system and techniques, the methodology and effectiveness have evolved with the help, love, and feedback of relationships/experiences I've had over the past 30 years. These have included different communication scenarios, concerns, physical differences, responses to stimulation, testing, and lessons learned. The male perspective provided valuable lessons of what to do and not because a penis fluctuates in size at random times and pulsates during orgasms. To develop a proven solution for introducing anal sex, it is helpful to have been in different relationships with women whose views on the topic were, "NO WAY you're going in there!" or "that's never going to happen, please lose my number!" Most women I've dated (90 %) had this initial reaction. These women felt that way because they had tried it before with a flawed process, heard it's painful, the hygiene factor, or thought it's taboo or forbidden.

After experiencing this method, these same women grew to love the caring, trust-building, and pleasurable process across multiple nights and led them to crave the intense orgasms from anal sex. These women are the book's most prominent supporters because the process focuses on patience, compassion, and is all about their pleasure. They inspired me to innovate, they provided their feedback to make sure the process/techniques felt good, and they helped further my purpose of helping women and couples around the world enjoy this sexual delight. Therefore, the advice is from a couple's perspective.

The immense work invested in authoring this book was to make a positive difference in peoples' sex lives.

Why a new release?

Over the last decade, I continued to create new techniques that led to an even more pleasurable experience throughout the system, especially in the entry process. From feedback on the improved process, it was recommended that I update the book with the new pleasuring techniques. There are more illustrations, and the 82 instructional illustrations have been redrawn by new artists. And there are new toys and lubes in Chapter Four.

I continued to conduct research, and on a warm spring day during the first COVID-19 lockdown, I discovered scientific studies that found anal sex enables women to have more and stronger orgasms. Therefore, I embarked on a master's-level research project. Well, it felt like it, from the number of resources I studied (resources listed above in - Isn't this information online for free). After reviewing the content and studies, I compiled the most compelling research in Section 1.6 with all sources linked. Also, more research is incorporated throughout the book. No other resources present this disparate data in one location. Therefore, I revamped the book with the research and my new techniques to help couples with a better system and scientific data to provide more credibility of anal sexuality's ability to give intense pleasure and orgasms!

What makes my content unique?

I combine creativity and lessons from extensive research in various subjects to formulate a unique solution with a woman's pleasure at heart. This book combines sexuality, psychology, physiology, neuroscience, and toys to provide a pleasurable solution. In my new book, Sex On A New Level, I combine those five topics with design, music, foods, drinks, props, construction, and technology to create sexual experiences. Since creating new experiences is a deep passion for me, not work, I am sharing over three decades of research, creations, and the art of my soul. As I stated earlier, I have a career that's not in the sex industry. I had to dedicate many nights and weekends to make a difference for others. If I can do the following:

- Help women not go through a bad experience but instead have a great anal sex experience and the most explosive orgasms of their lives.
- Help men enjoy anal sex with their partner and all the hot sex that comes with it, and provide stimulation techniques to give her the strongest orgasms ever with you.
- Prevent couples from having problems in their relationship because the man keeps asking for anal, but the woman is scared and gets frustrated at his requests.
- Introduce novelty into a couple's love life and a deeper connection.

Then the years of work have been worth it. I hope the research, stimulation techniques, and process are helpful.

Your feedback is valued.

Go to the Resources section to learn how to provide your feedback to improve the book and get rewarded for it. Providing your feedback will improve the content and help others. Enjoy!

Chapter One

Introduction

The Erotic Pleasure This Book Will Give You and Your Lover

1.1 The What and The How
The pleasure promise

This book demonstrates scientific research that shows women have more and stronger orgasms from anal sex. The content provides a proven, pleasurable, and caring method to arouse a woman's body and mind so she can experience her ultimate orgasms and sexuality, especially through anal stimulation. This is a detailed step-by-step guide that gradually and painlessly enables couples to enjoy the pleasures of anal sexuality. It contains illustrations with explanations that demonstrate what to do and how to take it slow while building trust with her so she experiences only pleasure. The content will address:

- Psychological and physical concerns
- Communication
- Building trust
- Strategy—how to give her exciting pleasure, one small step at a time
- Preparation for anal sex
- The right toys to use
- Lube comparisons

- Hygiene and techniques to feel, smell, taste, and be deliciously clean
- Advanced techniques—Thrilling cunnilingus, vaginal and anal play techniques and positions for hot erotic experiences

1.2 Why
The unmet need to provide a comprehensive and illustrated guide to anal pleasure

After reviewing other resources on the market, I realized a comprehensive painless introduction solution that built pleasure and trust over multiple days for women was missing. Other books have great information on:

- The history of anal sex
- In-depth anatomy of the anus
- Different types of anal acts
- Anal health

The above is valuable information, but the most important solutions needed address:

- How to introduce anal sex sensually without discomfort?
- How to overcome a negative view towards anal sex?
- How to take care of the hygiene factor?
- What techniques will enable her to love the process because of the consistent and intense orgasms she'll experience?

The typical advice in other resources (books, articles, videos) on first time anal sex tell couples to use lots of lube, have her relax, and take it "slow." The content does not explain HOW to go slow; therefore, the process is ambiguous and is the reason why so many women still have bad first-time experiences. It is like telling someone to go slow on the freeway without providing a speed limit, someone's slow will be too fast, and an accident is bound to happen.

These resources do not have sufficient illustrations nor detailed instructions for a man to know exactly what to do to build trust and gradually escalate enjoyment. A thorough explanation on how to go

Chapter One

"slow" in a pleasurable manner is especially important when introducing anal sex, because if you mess up once, you probably won't get another opportunity! This is the story of many women who tried it but won't do it again because their partners went too fast, and it hurt! Ladies, have you ever had a friend with this story?

There's new research that shows women experience orgasms more consistently and have more powerful orgasms from anal sex. Yet, many women are not experiencing them because a proper introduction process is missing from the general sexual consciousness. I felt couples could benefit from a comprehensive guide to prepare them to build trust and introduce pleasurable, pain-free, anal sexuality into their love life.

Building trust is key, and you build it by arousing her with small steps across multiple nights. Without her trust, good techniques, and a patient process, you cannot achieve the results you desire. A woman needs to feel secure that her partner knows how to introduce anal pleasure without feeling anxiety from the possibility of pain. The content is presented in a manner to arouse a woman to desire to try anal play. It provides visual stimulation and a system that women can look forward to engaging in.

The method I propose to introduce anal stimulation is designed so a woman is inspired to want more after each step through stimulation, teasing, and holding back until next time. She'll enjoy the arousal process, end up loving the pleasure from anal arousal, and have intense orgasms while having deeply connected sex.

There is an easy way to assess solutions, just go to a bookstore with a couple of female friends, one who hasn't done anal and one who has. Review multiple books on the subject, and see which method is preferred.

What this resource is not. It's not a guide on all things anal sex. I didn't want to replicate good work already available. I list online resources on anal sex health and other topics in the Resources section. This book provides research on the science of anal pleasure, a detailed solution for the introduction-phase, AND thrilling advanced techniques so you can relish in a variety of vaginal and anal pleasures.

1.3 For Whom
Erotic delight for women and men

The content is designed for a woman who is curious or scared of trying anal stimulation and sex, has never tried it, or did try it, but it was a bad experience. Also, for a man who tried introducing anal sex to their partner, but it did not go well. However, he still wants to introduce anal sex into their love life in a manner that will feel good to her. Or he has not tried it but wants to. Moreover, for long-term couples that feel their sex life has become monotonous, they lost the intimacy they used to have and want to ignite their passion again.

Many people are curious, but many have psychological barriers, and some have health concerns. I address the prominent issues and provide solutions for those concerns. If the process I provide is performed with affectionate sensuality and erotic passion, a woman will experience highly emotional and profound pleasure.

Both partners will enjoy every session and create incredibly satisfying sexual experiences throughout the process because you will only do what she enjoys, never anything more. The process is about indulging in her ecstasy and loving the journey. Adding this sexual delight will make you both happier in your sex life because it more than doubles the number of activities to savor.

Anal play will spice up your love life and bring you closer if it is introduced right. If done wrong, it will bring regret, so do not just scan the content, dig in to the details. Once a woman starts experiencing the simultaneous stimulation of multiple erogenous zones, she'll be aroused into having explosive full-body orgasms with you!

1.4 The Solution and Benefits
All the HOT rewards you will experience

The solution is not about trying to convince a woman to do anal by talking her into trying it. Though good communication part of the procees, solution is to arouse and pleasure her body and mind simultaneously to provide consistent and amazing stimulation to take her from "no way that's going to feel good" or "maybe" to "OMG that feels incredible!!!" In summary, the benefits of loving to pleasure patiently throughout the process and anal play are:

1. Provide a lot of erotic fun for both partners.
2. Give women the most incredible orgasms of their lives from anal sexuality and arousing multiple erogenous zones.
3. Enable a man to pleasurably introduce a woman to love anal sexuality and enjoy all of the hot sex that comes with it.
4. Significantly increase the sense of novelty and excitement in your love and sex life.
5. Reach a very deep level of intimacy and passion.
6. It more than doubles a couple's sexual activities and provides exciting new techniques for oral, anal, and vaginal arousal.
7. Build better trust and communication in your sex life.

1.5 The Difference

The pleasurable difference she'll feel and what makes this book unique

The philosophy and strategy here have a woman's best interest at heart. The content focuses on her experience. If she has a bad experience, then both of you will never revel in the ecstasy provided by anal sex because she won't try it again. The process is not just about technique but also about creating a sensual and emotional connection. If she receives incredible physical pleasure and has a deeply emotional experience, then she'll love it.

Women want you to remember the instructions since it will be their pain if you do not follow the process. Keep in mind that if it were your preventable pain on the line, you would want to ensure that the instructions are memorized and adhered to. So I have provided visual instructions to demonstrate what to do and help you remember the techniques. Thus, the summaries and illustrations will enable you to learn and review quickly.

What makes this book unique:

1. Research and science on **why women have more and stronger orgasms with anal stimulation.**
2. **An effective strategy that arouses her body and seduces her mind by using small steps that lead to anal pleasure.** You are not going to try it one night, but guide her through pleasurable steps that are procedural across multiple nights to build arousal and trust.
3. A detailed, step-by-step system that defines "how to take it slow," **The 7 Nights to Ecstasy System for beginners, The 3 Night Delight System for couples with anal play experience, and The Custom System for your specific situation.**
4. **A proven method** for associating pleasures that she already loves with anal stimulation, **the SEPOR Method.**
5. **82 Illustrations** that: a) communicate what to do and how; b) provide the content in a sensual and artistic fashion; and c) are designed to progressively arouse the female reader to try the anal play throughout the system.
6. My recommendations on the **best anal toys and lubes** (with 24 product images) and instructions on how to use them during the intro phase and advanced positions.
7. **Hygiene strategies** that will make preparation a hot experience.
8. **Advanced anal play and positions (26) with illustrations** and more detailed explanations than other resources.
9. Chapter **summaries for easy review.**
10. The **combination of the step-by-step system, number of instructional illustrations, arousal techniques, and entry techniques** are not in other books, DVDs, online videos, blogs, or web articles.

Chapter One

1.6 The Results Are In
Research shows women have more and stronger orgasms from anal sex. Growing awareness of its pleasure is increasing acceptance and engagement.

The following research shows women can experience easier, multiple, and powerful orgasms by including anal stimulation in their sex lives. Anal orgasms are real and intense. The research below (all sources are linked) will explain the following:

- How women orgasm more from anal stimulation than from intercourse.
- How engaging in more sexual acts increases the ability to have orgasms.
- Explain the physiology of anal pleasure.
- Illustrate how anal orgasms can be more powerful than vaginal orgasms.
- Provide evidence on increased engagement, interest, and acceptance of anal stimulation and sex.
- How stimulating her clitoris, G-spot, A-spot, U-spot, P-spot, K-spot, perineal sponge, cervix, other erogenous zones, and anus with multiple sex acts leads to the most explosive orgasms.

The research below spans various topics, therefore, scan the sections and only delve into the one's that peak your curiosity.

Women Orgasm More Frequently With Anal Sex

Research shows that from the women surveyed, of those that had anal sex, 94% orgasmed while only 66% orgasm during intercourse.*

FiveThirtyEight.com an ESPN owned, award-winning opinion poll site, published an article in August 2015 titled "The Gender Orgasm Gap (*source for statement in bold)." The article covered a 2009 study by the National Survey of Sexual Health and Behavior where 1,931 U.S.

adults aged 18 to 59 were asked about their most recent sexual experience (though the study is from 2009, this is data about the human body and sex, it doesn't lose its relevance today, it's not a study on social media trends that rapidly change, and no data has come out to refute its findings).

The study found that men are more likely to orgasm than women: 91% of men said they climaxed during their last sexual encounter compared with 64% of women. Interestingly, there were also differences between men and women regarding sexual acts that enabled them to orgasm. Men orgasmed around 90% of the time regardless of the type of sexual acts they participated in during a sex session. For women, only 66% reported orgasms during penile-vaginal intercourse, and 81% orgasmed when they received oral sex. The indisputable winner for women was receiving anal sex; 94% stated they orgasmed from anal sex. The data is plotted in the chart below.

How Come?

Share of respondents who achieved orgasm during their last sexual encounter, by type of sex act performed during encounter

SEX ACT	RESPONDENTS MEN	RESPONDENTS WOMEN	SHARE REACHING ORGASM
Partner masturbation	301	199	
Gave oral	377	315	
Received oral	457	263	
Penile-vaginal	830	730	
Received anal	25	31	
Gave anal	66	–	

FIVETHIRTYEIGHT — SOURCE: NATIONAL SURVEY OF SEXUAL HEALTH AND BEHAVIOR

Another interesting finding was that only 25 men and 31 women out of the 1,931 interviewed admitted that they had received anal sex during their last sexual encounter. If the study occurred today, and respondents were 100% honest, I believe the numbers would be much higher. While the number of women who admitted to having anal sex was only 31, the Central Limit Theorem in statistics states that a sample size of ≥30 is large enough for a distribution to be approximately normal. If people had a pleasurable introduction to anal sex, I believe the number of participants would be tremendously higher. As time passes, more people are disclosing

Chapter One

that they engage in anal sex. I will provide evidence of this in the sections to come.

Out of the 830 men who engaged in penile-vaginal intercourse, the number of men that reporting giving oral sex dropped to 377, a 55% decrease. Out of the 730 women that had penile-vaginal intercourse, the number of women that reported giving oral sex dropped to 315, a 57% decrease. People, people, people, PLEASE give more oral! Men reported receiving more oral sex than women, 457 stated they received oral sex while only 263 women stated receiving oral sex. If 81% of the women orgasmed from receiving oral, then they are not receiving as much oral as they should. The numbers show that both men and women need to give significantly more! People should make it their passion and art to give to their partners. Both sexes will have more incredible experiences when you love giving. In this book, giving oral is a vital component of the process.

Variety Leads to More People Reaching Climax

In a follow-up question, (chart below), people who engaged in five sexual acts, had the highest rate of climax, 97% of men and 89% of women stated they orgasmed from engaging in five sexual acts.

According to the sex acts listed in the sex acts chart, when the respondents engaged in five sexual acts, one of the five was anal sex (regardless of sequence). Therefore, more people indirectly disclosed anal sex activity

Variety Is The Spice Of Life
Share of respondents who achieved orgasm during their last sexual encounter, by the number of sexual acts performed

NUMBER OF SEX ACTS	RESPONDENTS		SHARE REACHING ORGASM
	MEN	WOMEN	
1	384	381	Women ~55%, Men ~90%
2	181	149	Women ~62%, Men ~85%
3	118	90	Women ~78%, Men ~88%
4	185	128	Women ~80%, Men ~90%
5	99	64	Women ~89%, Men ~97%

FIVETHIRTYEIGHT — SOURCE: NATIONAL SURVEY OF SEXUAL HEALTH AND BEHAVIOR in this question with 99 men and 64 women reporting engaging in five sexual acts. Both totals are more than sufficient for statistical validity.

A problem uncovered from this study is that many people are keeping it too basic. When men were asked how many sexual acts they engaged in during their last sex encounter, the number of men that responded more than one act decreased by greater than 50% from 384 to 181; and the number of women who engaged in more than one sexual act decreased by greater than 60% from 381 to 149. Come on now, this is a sad state of affairs considering that data shows more variety equals more orgasms!

In summary, the charts illustrate that engaging in five sexual acts gives couples the best likelihood of orgasm and that women orgasm significantly more from anal sex. Many people may not admit to having anal sex because it has been a taboo topic. Despite social shyness, the number of people interested and engaging in anal sex has increased over time as more people discover its ability to provide easier, multiple, and stronger orgasms for women. The evidence to come, will support this point.

AskMen Magazine also published the same report as 538 with an article in August 2015 called "Women Who Have Anal Sex More Likely to Orgasm." WellandGood.com, a woman-founded magazine covering the health and wellness industry, also covered the study with an article in October 2019 called, "A Human Sexuality Professor Believes Anal Sex Could Help Close the Orgasm Gap." In the article Dr. Zhana Vrangalova, LELO "sexpert" and NYU professor of human sexuality states, "Yes, I think anal play can play an important role in closing the orgasm gap, but only if done right."

Anal Orgasms Do Happen

Several health and lifestyle publications have reported that anal orgasms are real. **Women's Health magazine** published two articles on anal orgasms with similar titles, "Yes, Anal/Butt Orgasms Are Real: Here's How to Have One," one in January 2016 and the other in August 2018. In the 2018 article, Dr. Sheila Loanzon, an OB/GYN and fellow of the American College of Obstetrics and Gynecology, explains that orgasms are essentially a sudden release of sexual tension and how there are different ways that an orgasm can be reached, including anally. There are nerves that run from the anterior wall of the rectum to the vagina,

Chapter One

which enables arousal to occur from anal stimulation. Plus, the clitoris has "legs" that extend back into the anus.

Healthline magazine published an article in November 2019 called "5 Types of Orgasms and How to Get One or More." This credible health publication article states that the anal orgasm is one of the five a woman can have. The article was reviewed by Janet Brito, Ph.D., Certified Sex Therapist.

PJurLove, which produces sexual lubricants, presented an article in July 2018 titled "Anal Orgasms—Myth or Reality?" The article states that women who have anal penetration, are not just aroused in the anal area, the stimulation is felt in the vaginal region and even throughout the entire pelvic area. Also, that women have a particularly good chance of enjoying an anal orgasm if their G-spot or clitoris is stimulated at the same time as their anus.

Once a woman has passed the introductory stage, women can have powerful anal orgasms without direct stimulation of her clitoral head. This is definitely true from my experience. **RedBookMag.com**, a lifestyle magazine, published an article in 2017 titled, "All the Ways Women Can Orgasm Besides Touching Their Clits," where Steve McGough, Associate Professor of clinical sexology at the Institute for Advanced Study of Human Sexuality, explains how this can happen.

"It appears there are three things going on. Anal stimulation arouses the sacral nerve. Stimulating the anus causes the bulbocavernosus reflex to fire. (This is a reflex from the spine, like if you hit your knee.) If you stimulate the anus, this reflex will cause the clitoris to move or contract. (Conversely, if you stimulate the clitoris, the anus will contract.) So you may be stimulating the clitoris to some degree indirectly from this reflex."

Bustle.com is an online American women's magazine that positions news and politics alongside articles about beauty, celebrities, and fashion trends. In 2016, the magazine reached 50 million monthly readers. In April 2015, it distributed an article titled, "Are Anal Orgasms Real? Hell Yes, and Here Are 6 Ways to Get There." In the article, a sex education author and an adult film actress addressed the topic.

The first author, Patricia Johnson, co-author of *Partners in Passion, Great Sex Made Simple, Tantra for Erotic Empowerment,* and *The Essence of Tantric*

Sexuality, states the following: "Whatever your gender, the anus, and rectum are part of your sexual apparatus; the nerves and musculature are connected, and anal, rectal, and perineal stimulation all affect the genitals, both directly and indirectly. In women, anal penetration stimulates the erectile tissue in the lower part of the vagina and the G-spot."

The second author, Jillian Janson, an adult film actress, states, "Yes, it's possible, because I get them all the time! It usually is an extremely intense feeling. So it's really amazing having anal sex since there are multiple ways you can get pleased!" Jenny Block, author of *O Wow: Discovering Your Ultimate Orgasm*, writes, "Some of the very best orgasms that women report are called blended orgasms. That's when there is vaginal and anal penetration, as well as clitoral stimulation. There are all kinds of serious nerve endings in the anus."

In my experience, (DeCitore) in addition to exciting her G-spot from anal sex, different angles of penetration can stimulate her perineal sponge, K-spot, or other erogenous zones. The right dirty talk can also excite a woman to have an intense orgasm from anal penetration alone. Experimenting with her favorite anal sex positions and penetration angles will help her reach her pleasure potential. I provided additional articles in the Resources for Couples section at the end of the book.

Anal Orgasms Are More Intense

Many women that have anal orgasms state that they are extremely powerful and can even be more powerful than vaginal orgasms. Women can have anal orgasms from anal sex alone, though additional stimulation to other erogenous zones will enhance the orgasm experience.

A study conducted in 1982 by Bohen, Held, Sanderson, and Ahlgren titled *The Female Orgasm: Pelvic Contractions*, found that women have stronger contraction pressure from anal orgasms than vaginal orgasms (displayed in the chart below).

Lioness.io, an innovative company that makes a "smart vibrator" that provides biofeedback data during use, has tested the intensity of a vaginal orgasm versus an anal one. The vibrator syncs to a phone app and provides data on the strength of an orgasm so users can track and improve their experiences. Co-founder and CEO Liz Klinger wrote an article in

Chapter One

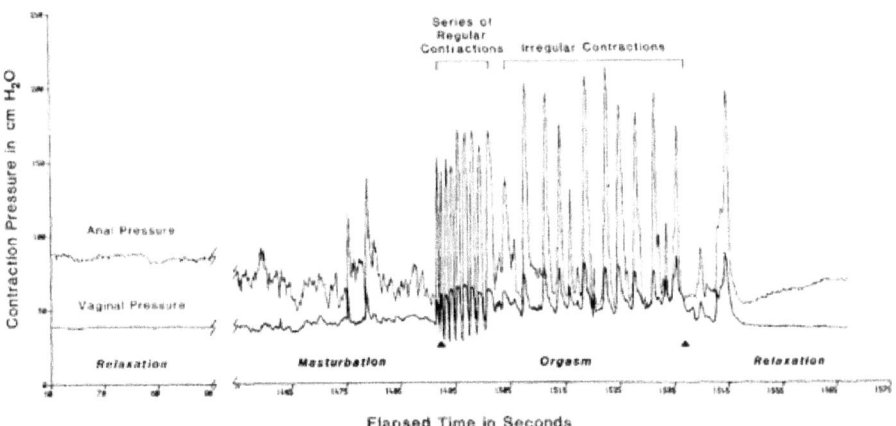

February 2019 entitled, "I DPed (double penetration) Myself to Prove that Asses and Vaginas do the Same Thing During Orgasm." As the title implies, she tested both orgasms and determined that both had the same pattern of contractions, although the anal orgasm had much stronger contractions. Below is the data from the article.

The pattern of body contractions may look similar between an anal

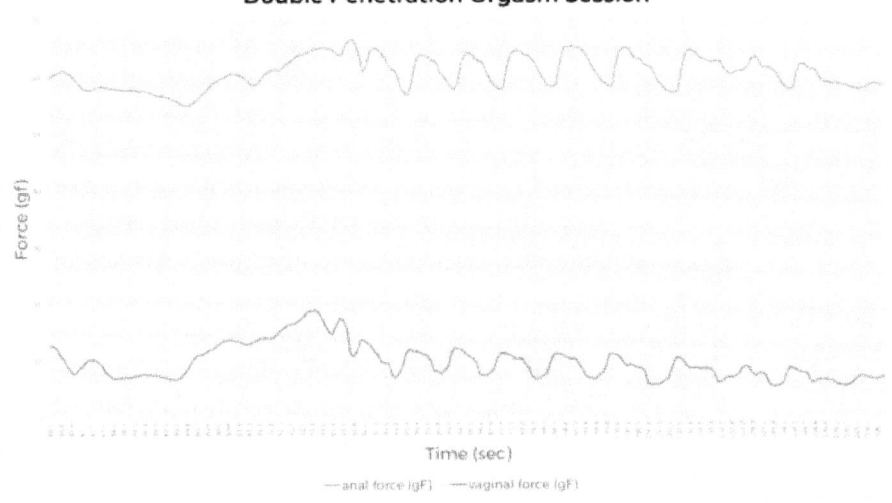

orgasm and a vaginal orgasm, but the anal orgasm was more than 4.5 times stronger than the vaginal orgasm. Klinger wrote, "The anal orgasm has a larger peak-to-peak amplitude, meaning those anal muscles relax and squeeze stronger than my vaginal muscles during orgasm."

The sphincters of the urethra and anus are considered a part of the deep pelvic floor muscle (PFMs) complex. The anal sphincter is made up of two parts. The external anal sphincter is a striated, or voluntary, muscle that we can actively contract and relax, whereas the internal anal sphincter is a smooth, or involuntary, muscle. Similarly, the urinary sphincter has two parts, one that is under voluntary control (what we commonly think of as the PFMs in general, which are striated muscles) and those of the urinary sphincter (which are smooth muscle)." Many online articles feature women corroborating Klinger's "research."

Health Line Magazine published an article in December 2016 titled "Does Anal Sex Have Any Benefits?" The article states, "Anal orgasms can be intense! That's because the anus is packed with loads of sensitive nerve endings, some of which are connected to the genitals. And that's not all! For ciswomen (assigned female at birth), anal sex can hit two hotspots: the G-spot and A-spot. Both are located along the vaginal wall but can be indirectly stimulated during anal. These spots have the potential to produce FULL-BODY orgasms. Rubbing them just right may even lead to female ejaculation, and the phenomenon referred to as 'squirting.' Yes, please!"

The Physiology of Anal Pleasure

How are women able to enjoy anal play, sex, and have orgasms? The answer lies in the anatomy of a woman's body, the proper stimulation of her anatomy, and the overall intimate experience that her partner gives her. Below are several explanations on the physiology of anal pleasure.

Health.com published an article in March 2019, titled "Anal Orgasms Are Real- Here's How to Have One." The article explains how anal orgasms happen. An anal O is the result of sexual stimulation of the nerves in and around the anus. "The anus is packed with nerves, especially the incredibly erogenous pudendal nerve—which connects to the clitoris," Megwyn White, director of education at online sex toy retailer Satisfyer, tells Health. The pudendal nerve carries sensation to and from your perineum, reaching your vagina, vulva, and anus.

What does this kind of orgasm feel like? Andrea Barrica, founder of the sexual education website **O.school**, tells Health that some women describe it as being similar to a clitoral orgasm—a pulse of pleasurable contractions, just around the anal sphincter. Others may feel more of a "spreading wave" of pleasure.

In a similarly titled article "Butt Orgasms Are REAL, Here's How to Have One," **Women's Health Magazine** provides another explanation on how anal orgasms happen. "The clitoris is shaped like a wishbone, and for many women, the clitoris extends down to the anus. During anal penetration, you're also stimulating the clitoral legs. An anal orgasm happens through indirect stimulation of a woman's G-spot through the wall shared between the vagina and rectum.

With all this stimulation going on, your chances of having an intense orgasm are good. In addition to the G-spot, there's another area located at the back of the deepest part of the vagina near the cervix (the A-spot, Anterior Fornix erogenous zone). When stimulated through the tissue that separates your vagina from your rectum, this location can produce intense orgasms.

Quora.com is an international, question-and-answer website where questions are asked, answered, and edited by Internet users. The question, "Can women reach an orgasm from anal sex?" was posted. Michael Reitano, Physician in Residence at Roman Health, answered the question with a good physiological explanation.

"The reason anal sex can be pleasurable is based on human anatomy and the pudendal nerve, which supplies the brain with sexual sensations from the pelvic region. The pudendal nerve (there are two of them, one on the right and one on the left) travels into the anogenital region within the pudendal canal, but it soon separates into branches. The first branch becomes the inferior rectal nerve and then the perineal nerve (which supplies sensation to that area between the genitals and the anus), eventually becoming the dorsal nerve of the clitoris in women and the dorsal nerve of the penis in males. It supplies sensation to the anal opening, the scrotum in men, and the labia in women. It is responsible for the swelling of the penis and the clitoris and is even responsible for the spasms of ejaculation."

"Sexual sensations are not limited to the very specifically located regions most people think about. In fact, the clitoris extends from the small external organ with which people become intimately familiar (hopefully), but run internally far into the body along areas near the vaginal wall."

"The sexual sensations that may occur with stimulation of any of these nerves in these various locations can be unique and for some pleasurable."

In the article "Are Anal Orgasms Real? Hell Yes, And Here Are 6 Ways To Get There," from **Bustle.com**, it states, "stimulation of the anus, perineum, and rectum can engage the pelvic and pudendal nerves, which are implicated in the orgasmic response. The pudendal nerve also supplies the genitals with nerves and is thought to be most central to orgasm. The pelvic nerve connects the cervix, uterus, and prostate to the brain, and the hypogastric nerve relates to the vagina, cervix, and rectum. The role of the vagus nerve is less well understood, though research over the past decade has shown that some women with completely severed spinal cords can still experience orgasm and that the vagus nerve is the pathway," says Patricia Johnson, co-author of Partners in Passion, Great Sex Made Simple, Tantra for Erotic Empowerment, and The Essence of Tantric Sexuality.

The anatomical make up of the body enable women to have intense anal orgasms. Now you just have to learn how to stimulate her mind, body, and soul in the right manner to experience them.

More Couples Are Having Anal Sex

NY Magazine published an article in December 2006 titled "The Bottom Line." The article states that the Centers for Disease Control's National Survey of Family Growth (2005) found that anal sex is rapidly becoming a regular feature of heterosexual couples' horizontal activities. The survey showed that 38% of men between 20 and 39 and 33% of women ages 18 to 44 engage in heterosexual anal sex. Compare that with the CDC's 1992 National Health and Social Life Survey, which found that only 26% of men 18 to 59 and 20% percent of women 18 to 59 indulged in it.

The **National Center for Biotechnology Information** (NCBI) released a study titled "Heterosexual Anal and Oral Sex in Adolescents and Adults in the United States, 2011-2015." The results state that overall, of women 15 to 44 years old, 33% tried anal sex (of a sample size of 11,152). Among the age group of 25 to 34, 40% had tried it. For the men, 38% of individuals between 15 to 44 years old (sample size 9,218) had ever engaged in anal sex. The age group of 20 to 24-year-olds featured the highest percentage at 46%.

Chapter One

Women's Health magazine presented an article in August of 2015 titled "A Breakdown of the Women Most Likely to Try Anal Sex." The article analyzed data from the National Survey of Family Growth and looked at a nationally representative sample of 10,463 straight, sexually active women between the ages of 15 and 44. Researchers discovered that 36% of the women surveyed said they had tried anal sex at least once in their lives and 13% had anal sex in the last year.

Womanlab.org, an online sexual wellness magazine geared towards women, published an article in May 2018 titled, "The What and Why of Anal Sex," which reported that 30-40% of heterosexual Americans have had anal sex, though many researchers think this number is underreported.

What countries are having the most anal sex and why?

DrFelix.com, a health site for men and women, published an article titled "Having Sex, from Chile to China. that answered the question." The article reports on sexual behavior around the world and states that the country that has the most anal sex is Greece, with 55% of the men and women having tried anal sex at least once. Other countries that are also highly active in anal sex are Chile, Italy, and Croatia.

Statista.com reports that in 2014, Greece had the most sex out of all the countries with an average of 164 sexual encounters per year per person. The reason for this stat can be because Greece takes more time to socialize for fun and is obviously sexually open to new activities. Compared to a country like Japan, which has the least sex, probably since it is highly work-oriented, people spend less time socializing with the opposite sex, and people are less open to sexual exploration. Results from a Durex survey show that only 20% of respondents reported being open-minded about their sex life, with the average for 41 countries at 45%. This can be a precursor to boredom, 13% of Japanese respondents reported their sex is monotonous, with the average across all countries at 7%.

This is an example on a national level that shows when people are not open-minded to trying new things, it leads to a monotonous sex life, which leads to less sex. As covered earlier, variety is the spice of life, and including anal in your sexual repertoire can lead to wanting to have sex more because there is more ways to enjoy variety.

Her Ultimate Pleasure

The number of people interested and engaging anal sexuality has increased significantly compared to a couple of decades ago. The research in the last two sections reveal the increase, but many people are still hesitant to admit to having anal sex. Despite a growing percentage of women are engaging in anal sex, lack of good instruction on how to introduce anal sexuality is stifling higher numbers. There a variety of other indicators to show the increase in interest and social acceptance, such as the number of Internet searches, topics viewed on adult sites, number of YouTube videos on the topic, increase in anal toy sales, and the number of popular magazines covering the topic.

More People Are Searching on the Topic

People are highly interested in searching for the term "anal." A Google Trends report from 2004 to the present indicated that on average the term "anal" has a higher search frequency than popular searches like those for the stock market, Beyoncé, Kim Kardashian, and cooking. Beyoncé and Kim K. had periodic spikes above the term "anal," for instance, when Kim K. "broke the Internet" in November 2014. Searches for the stock market had a huge spike during the COVID-19 pandemic. For clarification, search results for the term "anal" do not include when the word is combined with another to form a phrase with an entirely new meaning, like "anal itching." The results are for the term on its own, which is usually understood to be shorthand for anal sex.

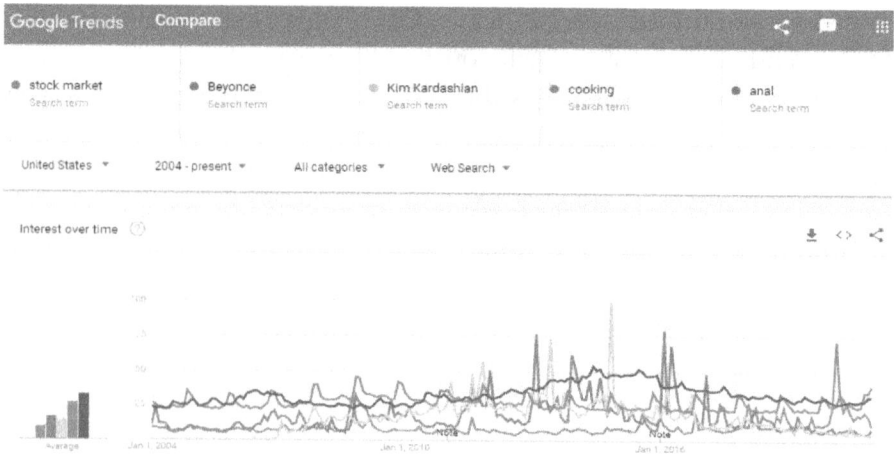

In the chart below, the frequency of a search for "anal" is about two-thirds as popular as the frequency for the term "XXX."

Chapter One

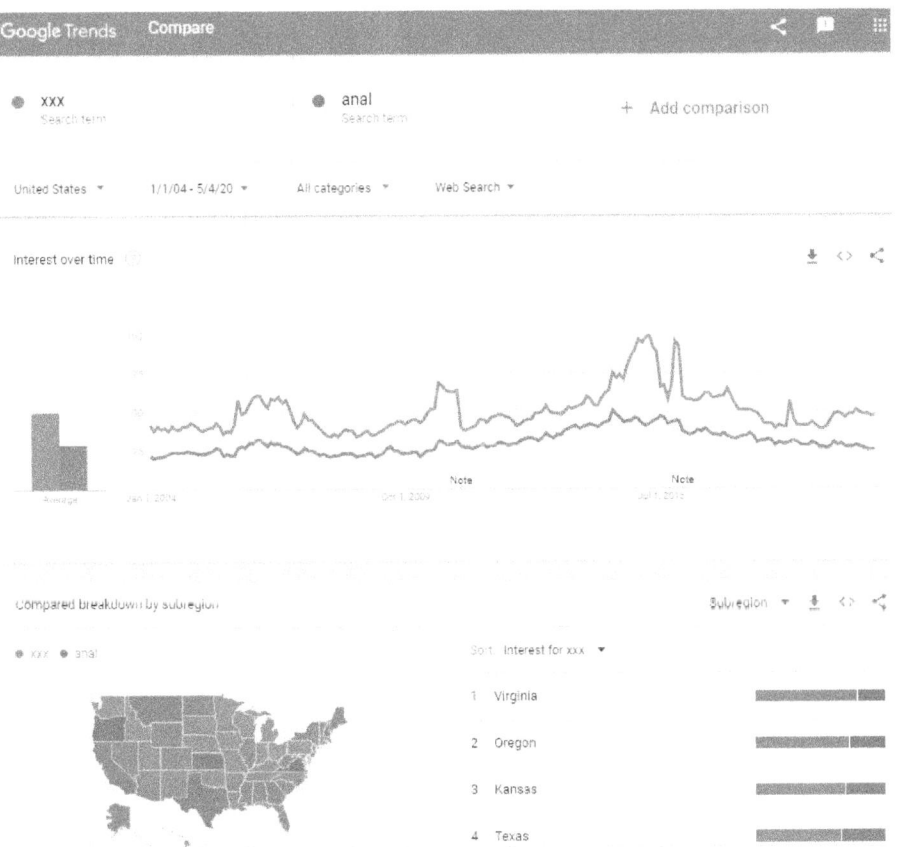

You might think these searches are largely performed by men. However, Men's Health published an article entitled, "Pornhub Just Dropped Some VERY Interesting Stats About Women's Porn Habits." The 2019 study identified women's top searched-for terms, and anal was one of the only three sexual acts searched for, the others being cream pie and lesbian scissoring. The other top terms were hentai and descriptions of women such as ebony, Asian, and Latina. None of the top terms were gentle sex, oral sex, massage, kissing, or romantic sex which are some of the top sex acts that women want as reported by Forbes or rough sex, squirting, bondage, threesome, or double penetration as reporting by Pornhub's Popular With Women article.

PornHub Insights, a publication division that provides statistical research on search trends, published a report titled "What Women Want." It provided an accompanying chart identifying the top categories women and men prefer. It was no surprise that anal was in the top 5 categories for men since it commonly stated as a top desired sexual act. What was a

Her Ultimate Pleasure

surprise is that anal was #8 for women. I believe it would be higher still if, again, they knew about a good introduction system.

A follow-up segment, "More of What Women Want," illustrates categories viewed more by women compared to men. The chart below shows out of 15 categories, "double penetration" (anal and vaginal penetration) is ranked #8 and grew by 87% from the previous year's study. Other categories that tend to incorporate anal sex are gangbangs, threesomes, and orgies, which are all part of the top 15 categories.

Top Categories Viewed by Men and Women
Lesbian
Gay (male)
Teen
For Women
Ebony
MILF
Squirt
Anal
Mature
Big Dick
Threesome
Big Tits
Gangbang
Rough Sex
Hentai
Bondage
Teen
MILF
Mature
Ebony
Anal
Lesbian
Gay (male)
Big Tits
Amateur
Squirt
Big Dick
Hentai
BBW
Asian
Creampie
Threesome

CATEGORIES VIEWED MORE BY WOMEN COMPARED TO MEN
Pornhub
REDTUBE
For Women +202%
Lesbian +155%
Solo Male +135%
Hardcore +113%
Rough Sex +106%
Gangbang +104%
Bondage +91%
Double Penetration +87%
Toys +69%
Gay (male) +60%
Threesome +54%
Bisexual +53%
Fisting +46%
Orgy +33%
Squirt +28%
pornhub.com/insights

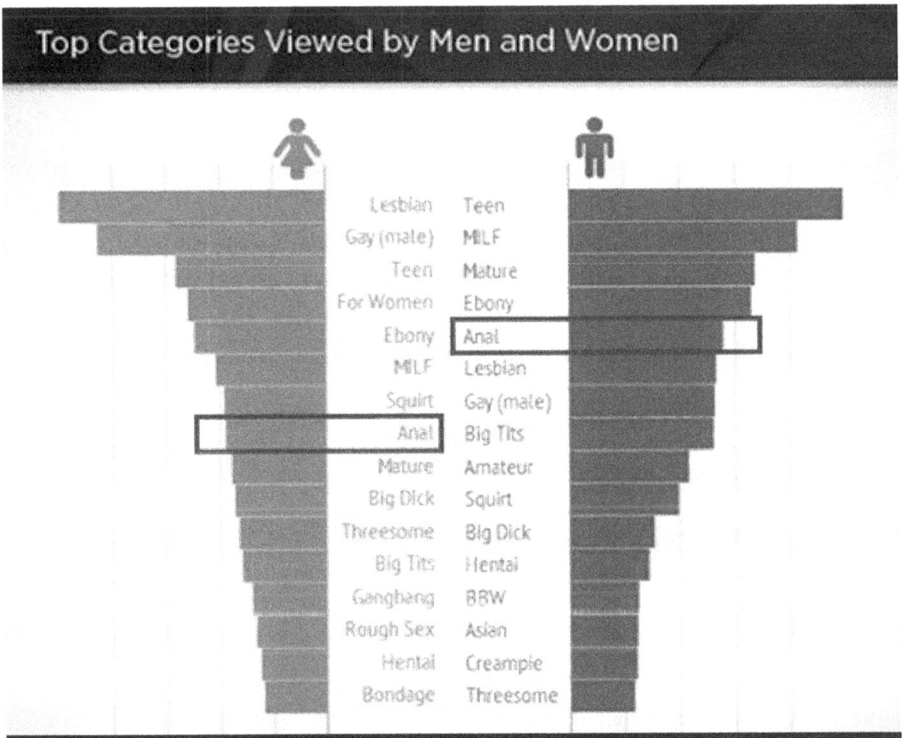

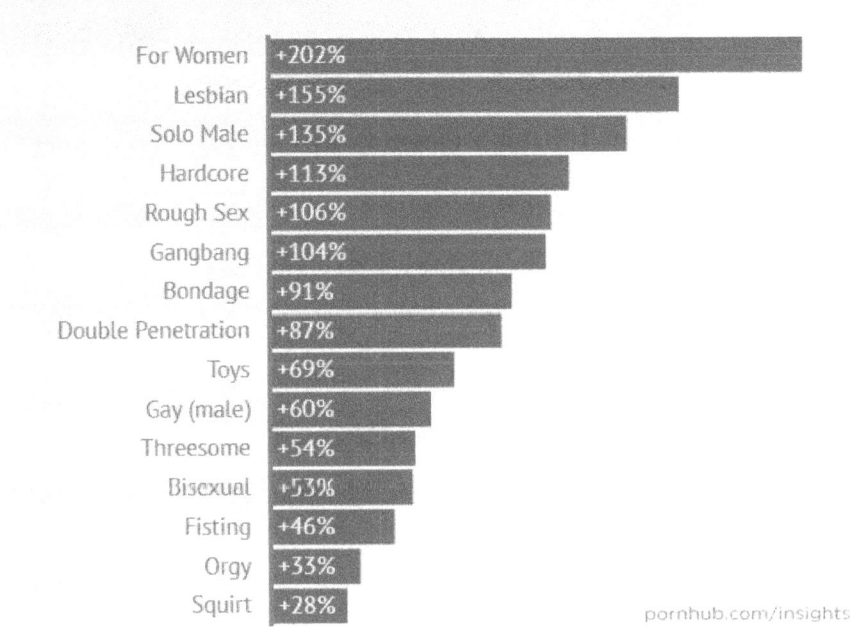

Popular Magazines Increased Their Coverage of the Topic

A tremendous indicator that anal sex is penetrating the social consciousness is the number of popular and credible magazines that are writing articles on the topic. Major magazines on health focused on women, pop culture, lifestyle, fitness, and psychology have written articles on anal sex. Here is a list of articles to scan from popular magazines that shows that awareness is building about the pleasure of anal sex for women.

Cosmopolitan: The 23 Biggest Misconceptions About Anal Sex

Shape: Best Anal Sex Toys

Women's Health Mag: Anal Sex Guide

Glamour: Anal Sex

MarieClaire: Rise in Anal Sex Statistics

Allure: Beginner Butt Plug Anal Play Advice

Self: Starter Anal Sex Toys

Health: The 5 Best Anal Sex Positions for Women

HealthLine: How to Have an Anal Orgasm: 35 Tips for You and Your Partner

Psychology Today: Introducing a Different Kind of Play into Partner Sex

Vogue: Is Anal Sex No Longer Taboo

Goop (by Gwyneth Paltrow) : Reality Check- Anal Sex

Harper's Bazaar and People Mag on Gwyneth Paltrow's Guide to Anal Sex.

Mens Health: How Many Women Are Having Anal Sex

Ask Men: Women Who Have Anal Sex Are More Likely to Orgasm

GQ: A History of Anal Sex

Chapter One

Insider: 9 Questions About Anal Sex You've Been Too Afraid to Ask - Answered

Female Empowerment is Improving the Quality of Sex

I believe the rise of female empowerment has improved the quality of sex. Throughout history and even up to the mid 19th century, women had to put up with lousy sex experiences because men were the predominant providers. If sex was lackluster and pleasure was one-sided, they could not just walk out because the majority did not have opportunities available to survive independently. As ideologies about equal rights and legislation have progressed, women have attained the opportunities to demonstrate that they are powerful business, political, and humanitarian leaders and proven to be better managers.

No longer do women have to stay in an unsatisfactory relationship for any reason, including sex. Women are empowered to take control of their happiness and pleasure. They are confident in their ability to lead change, provide for themselves and their families, feel great about their bodies, and are empowered to pleasure themselves and their lover. Now that there is a greater balance of power, a man has to pay more attention to how well he sexually satisfies his wife or lover. Women have the power to say no or yes to any sexual experience. If they stated they have anal orgasms, it's because they were in a sexual experience where they felt comfortable and pleasured by choice. Therefore, the increase in anal sex coverage, especially by female managed or owned publications, is because they are leading those conversations and are genuinely experiencing pleasure.

Moreover, online/app dating services such as Match, OkCupid, Bumble, and Tinder provide a large selection of people to date. Options are vast for both partners, but especially for women. Statista.com reports as of June 2020, Tinder's user base is 72% male and 28% female. In addition, both partners can see what other people do during sex on adult sites that show real couples having sex, not professional porn actors, so that they can compare their experience versus others.

All of the above increases the necessity for men to be more skilled at relationships and sexual dynamics to keep a union healthy and satisfied, whether short-term or long-term because women can easily find a new partner. Although dating apps provide females an advantage, men also have access to a greater selection of females to date. Both partners have an abundance of options at their fingertips. Therefore, it is essential for both to view sexual and relationship knowledge as art and science; and that they need to continuously learn and create novelty to keep their love lives happy and exciting.

People of Faith Are Also Enjoying More Sexual Acts

Another reason why people are hesitant to engage in anal play is due to religious restrictions. However, more people of faith are engaging in a variety of sexual acts. According to an article published by PsychologyToday called, "Religion & Sexuality: Iron Age or Dark Ages?" written by Marty Klein, Ph.D., certified sex therapist and licensed psychotherapist, he states that guidelines about sex were formulated and distributed primarily between 1,200 B.C.E. and 800 C.E. The following acts were stated to be intrinsically evil and therefore, were always immoral, regardless of circumstances, intention, or purpose:*

1. no sex before marriage
2. no birth control (condom, female contraceptive, IUD, or surgery)
3. no masturbation
4. no manual sex/stimulation (when a hand, finger, tongue, or other part of the body is used to please one's spouse)*
5. no oral sex
6. no sex with an object or device*
7. no sexual fantasy
8. no anal sex
9. no sex outside marriage (if a spouse passes or after divorce)
10. no sex during menstruation
11. no abortion
12. no same-gender sex
13. no sex with more than one partner*
14. no non-monogamy
15. no marrying outside the religion

These guidelines are from a list reported in an article called "Sexual Sins within Marriage" from Catechism.cc., (Point 2, examples).

Most people in the U.S., including people of faith, have partaken in at least one of the first six. KlTV.com reports that "95% of Americans have had pre-marital sex". For the remaining 5%, if you ever masturbated, manually stimulated their spouse, had oral sex, or used a toy, then I imagine that increases the percentage of people that have engaged in one or more of those acts to at least 99% of the U.S. population. PRNewswire.com reports that 92% of American men masturbate, and "78% of people do on a global scale". In an article called "The State of Oral Sex in America" by BeSpokeSurgical.com, reported that a 2019 survey of 1008 U.S. citizens above 18 years old, showed 80.7% stated oral sex is pleasurable. At least that percentage is having oral sex, the actual percentage is higher since there were other answers with "yes" selected. Statista.com reported that 78% of women own a vibrator.

According to the C.D.C., 95% of women have used a male condom for contraception. As for manual stimulation of your partner during sex, (use of a hand, finger, or tongue anywhere to please your partner, such as breasts or genital area), there are no stats that I could find on manual stimulation/sex engagement. I imagine that it is such a ubiquitous act that it would be above 99%. So if you did any of the above activities, congratulations, you are a human, trying out human needs and desires. Trying something new can be valuable to maintain a happy relationship and keep your sex life fulfilling.

Doctor Klein, from PsychologyToday, states, "To put this in context, when these (primarily western world) restrictions were developed the people involved:

* expected to live, if things went well, to about age 40; (shorter relationships)

* had almost no privacy;

* had no electricity, and virtually no light after dark;

* had very little non-family mixed-gender interaction;

* had no indoor plumbing, and rarely bathed;

"The idea that we in the 21st century would live according to rules set up by people living in such extraordinarily different circumstances is bizarre. Do modern people want to be limited to the medical, agricultural, or industrial knowledge of a thousand or two thousand years ago? No? Then why do three billion men and women today limit their sexual expression to the behaviors, beliefs, superstitions, and fear of the people during those times?"

How many people of faith are engaging in oral or anal sexuality and are willing to admit it?

The Institute for Family Studies (IFStudies.org) published a study on the sexual activity of 4,969, never-married, evangelical young people, between 15 to 22, with 51% female and 49% male. The average percentage of females that engaged in oral sex in the age group between 18 to 22 across Evangelical Protestants, Mainline Protestants, Black Protestants, and Catholics was 69.5% for females and 71% for males. Engaging in anal sex was 21.75% for females and 18.75% for males. Consider maybe not all were honest. Those percentages are probably higher today, with more mainstream magazines covering new sexual research on a variety of proven paths to a happier sex life.

UncoveringIntimacy.com, a Christian Life and Marriage site, surveyed 260 members regarding anal play and sex. For the question, "Do you practice anal play in your marriage?" 47% of respondents stated yes. Remember, only a sample size of 30 is needed to start forming a normal bell curve. Religious adults married for 10 to 14 years reported the highest engagement in anal play.

Finally, ChristianPost.com published an article called "Christian Couples Engaging in Kinky Sex, Including 'Anal Play,' Say It's OK if It's in Heterosexual Marriage." The article covers the book Christians Under Cover: Evangelicals and Sexual Pleasure on the Internet. The book's research focused on tens of thousands of Christians who sought sexual guidance, were heterosexual, married, monogamous, and did not look at pornography.

Burke found in her study was that even within the confines of Protestant heterosexual norms, Christians still found creative ways to explore a cornucopia of sexual interests. "For some, this means oral sex, anal sex, masturbation, the use of sex toys, the list could go on."

Vice channel, covered how Christian sex toy shops like Covenant Spice caters to sexual activity utilizing all orifices in marriage, including toys that promote "anal play as straight-friendly" for Christians. The husband and wife Christian owners of Covenant Spice provide the view below.

"We believe that sex between a husband and a wife is a gift from God, and is meant to be enjoyed in all of its wonder and passion. We believe that according to the scriptures, it is acceptable for a husband and wife to explore whatever options bring them pleasure as a married couple that do not cause harm, do not violate a scriptural command, and do not cause either spouse to be uncomfortable. We are aware that many things on this site may come as a surprise to someone from a traditional or more formal Christian background. We would encourage you to pray together as a couple and seek the Lord's wisdom."

This view seems to be more in line with the actual activities that are happening at home with religious couples. In conclusion, a very large majority of the population, including couples of faith, have engaged in a sex act that was deemed as forbidden a couple of thousand years ago. Trying something new just shows that you are human, curious, and that you want to keep your relationship alive. Today, technology has evolved, enabling us to maintain thorough cleanliness, dynamics of relationships have changed, women are empowered, and fostering a happy relationship or marriage is important to live a fulfilling life. Consider trying new activities that have been proven to provide immense pleasure if introduced in a caring manner.

Sales of Anal Sex Toys Are Up

Another important indicator that more people are engaging in anal sexuality is the increase in anal toy sales. Google Trends chart below shows that searches for butt plugs have increased since 2004.

Babeland has seen an increase in anal-related sales. Between 2012 and 2015, the genre averaged about 5% growth per year. Forbes published an article in March 2020 titled "People Are Using Self-Isolation To Try Out New Sex Toys." In the article, a spokesperson for Adam & Eve says, "We definitely think individuals and couples are self-soothing and looking for some de-stressors during these uncertain times. We've seen a jump in couples toys, and anal toys are quite popular." I alone might have contributed 1% of national sex toy sales! :)

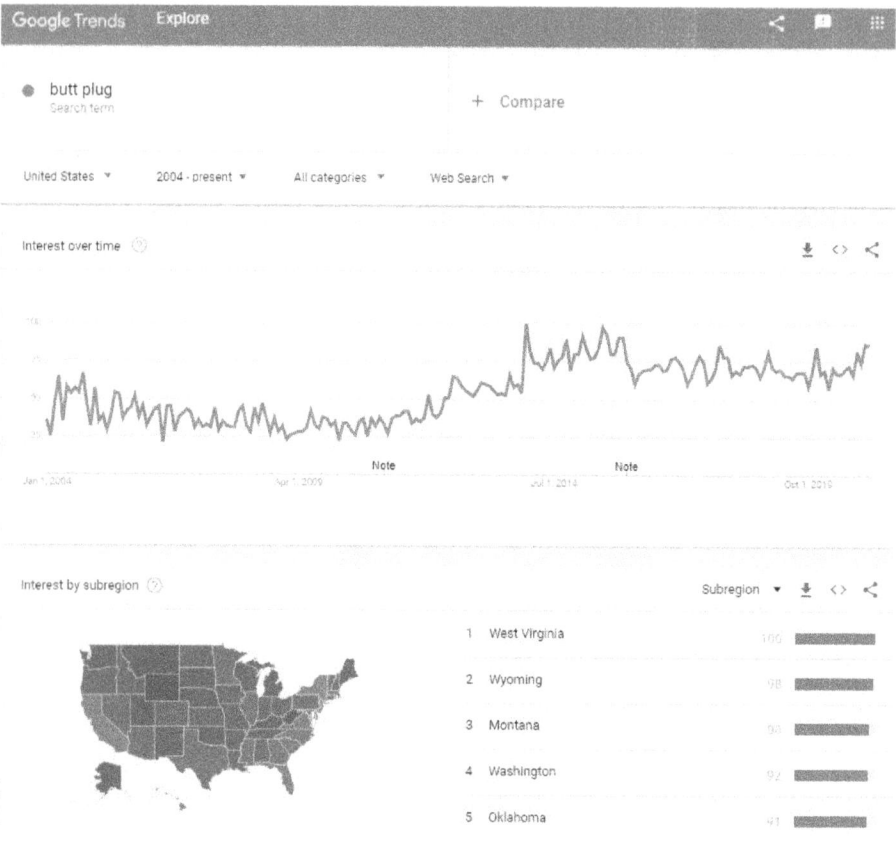

Increase in YouTube Videos on the Topic

More people are producing content about anal sex online to address the increased interest. As of the summer of 2020, there are over 500 YouTube videos on anal sex. A video posted in November 2019 on how to have anal sex currently has over 19 million views accumulated in a period of 7 months. The top 5 YouTube videos on anal sex have 38 million views and each has content on how to have anal sex. Clearly, millions of people are interested and clicking away to find a method so they don't get butt hurt. Click for yourself and compare solutions.

Chapter One

Anal Sex Reaches Other Levels of Soulful Experience and Releases Deep-Rooted Tension

Anal sex is also a way to reach deeper connections and release tension. In an article from Beducated.com titled "How to Raise Your Erotic Consciousness: Make Love On The 7 Chakras," the author discusses how Kundalini energy can be skillfully blasted through each chakra (energy center), purifying it and opening it up. Kundalini is a form of divine feminine energy believed to be located at the base of the spine in the root chakra. When awakened, it leads to spiritual liberation and the release of deep-rooted tension. Anal sex can do this for a woman. The article explains, when you make love on the root chakra, you tap into your most vital being; you tap into your body. The root chakra connects with the earth, with vital earth energy. Bring your awareness to your perineum (the space between the vagina and the anus) and imagine you are moving into your primal being, of your wild nature.

Sex on this chakra is raw. Express that in your bedroom. Touch each other firmly, squeeze each other's bodies. Have strong, powerful sex. Be wild, be bold, and don't care what others may think of you. Opening the root chakra means deciding to be inside your body while you make love, be in the now. Anal sex can be scary for many people, but it can create a lot of healing on this level.

TheSensousMistic.com posted an article titled "Anal Sex" by the Rev. Goddess Charmaine, where she states, "Opening my ass for pleasure purged the shit (bad thoughts) that no longer could keep me in bondage! All those thoughts that plagued me and forced me to believe that I wasn't pretty enough, that no one could love me, that I was going to hell, that I was crazy, flew out of me—and I was left with the clean consciousness of pure love. I accepted myself and received the correct information about my original blessing. I am born blessed! The level of shame that was released when I allowed myself to be deeply penetrated and paralyzed with pleasure shed light on the power of the body! I began a deeper path of realization once my ass accepted that lovely wand of delight. The pressure, the breathing, the sweating, and yes, oh yes, the prayer! Oh, God, oh God!!!"

Conclusion, Her Ultimate Pleasure Lies In Arousing Multiple Erogenous Zones, Including Anal Stimulation

There is a plethora of information dispersed across the Internet regarding this subject matter. Therefore, many people are not aware of the combined research, science, and orgasmic benefits of anal sex because there's not a single resource that has compiled the data for people. I have worked diligently to ensure that I provided you with information that has been vetted or provided by credible sources and professionals. Then, I assembled what I thought was the most compelling from 237 online articles in one location for you.

Anal orgasms have been described as intense, full-body experiences. I want to add my own spin on how to enhance the orgasmic experience. If you stimulate multiple erogenous zones simultaneously and she exercises her Kegel muscles, you can give her the most explosive orgasms.

By stimulating at least three or more erogenous zones, along with creating an intense emotional and connected experience, she'll have incredibly powerful orgasms. The core three are her clitoris, G-spot, and anus. Combine and mix the stimulation for as many of the following as you can, her <u>clitoris, G-spot, U-spot, A-spot, Cervix, P-spot, K-spot, perineal sponge</u>, anus, breasts, neck, lips, ass cheeks, her senses, and emotions. I cover these spots in more detail in Night Three of the Seven Night Ecstasy system. You can arouse these spots with finger play from both hands while you have sex with her, your penis, and your mouth, or with toys that can add their own stimulation, thereby freeing your hands to give pleasure to other parts of her body.

In regards to her incorporating Kegel exercises, PsychologyToday reported in an article titled, <u>Want More Intense Orgasms? Try This Simple, Subtle Exercise</u>, Kegels also enable stronger orgasms. In 1948, Arnold Kegel, M.D., developed Kegel exercises to help cure women's stress incontinence, but a beautiful by-product resulted. Many of his patients reported having more intense and pleasurable orgasms from doing the exercises. Since Kegel developed his exercises, many studies have demonstrated their effectiveness—for better orgasms. For example, In 2017, Iranian scientists worked with 145 menopausal women who complained of decreased sexual function and enjoyment. Some received standard medical care. Others attended a sex education class. And some attended the class and also practiced Kegels. After 12 weeks, the class/Kegel women reported the most erotic enhancement.

Women's Health Magazine published two articles that cover the topic. The first, How to Use Kegels to Make Your Orgasms Stronger, and the second, How to Have a Full-Body Orgasm. Article one states, these simple, unobtrusive exercises will strengthen and tone your vaginal muscles, which boosts your arousal both before and during sex. The result? Many who practice Kegels are able to climax in positions where they couldn't before, and some report being able to achieve multiple orgasms. Regularly exercising your vagina will also help you have more intense contractions during orgasm due to more blood being sent to your pelvic region. Your partner will benefit as well; Kegels will help you get a better grip during intercourse so you can hold tight onto your partner's penis.

Article two reported that one of the four tips to have full-body orgasms is to do Kegel exercises. There are many online articles on the subject. In regards to anal sex, Kegels help keep your sphincter muscles healthy and strong. More on the topic of Kegels for anal sex is provided in Chapter Five, Section 5.3 - Tips to Maintain Enjoyment.

Also, as stated in the research, variety in sexual acts enables women to orgasm more. You can give your partner multiple orgasms by alternating your focus on which spots to pleasure. You can include different pleasure spots with various sexual acts to give her orgasms in a variety of ways. For example, cunnilingus that includes U-spot, G-spot, and anal stimulation. Vaginal sex with stimulation of her U-spot, anal, A-Spot, Cervix, P-spot, G-spot, clitoris (of course) and other erogenous zone stimulation. Anal sex with stimulation of her clitoris, U-spot, G-spot, perineal sponge, and other erogenous zones. With toys and all of your body parts, you can arouse many of the spots at once. I will provide the finger play and toy techniques for you to implement throughout the "7 Nights to Ecstasy" system in chapter 5, Advanced Anal Play.

View the stimulation of all of these spots/zones as a musical artist. Each spot/zone makes a beautiful note of arousal (her moans, groans, gasps, yes's, and OMGs). You want to create an amazing song of her pleasure and yours. Every note has nuances, vibratos, bending, and how strong you play the notes makes different sounds, and the feeling that emanates from the notes is different when you hear them. Invent many different melodies and songs together by sequencing the notes differently, modifying how you play them. Inspire different vibes/feelings by the intensity of your emotions by tantalizing her with soft sensuality to fiery passion to intense erotic hunger. It is about enjoying playing the music, not getting to the end of the song. Musicians don't rush the end of a song with the end as the goal, they love every note of a song. They flow in the moment. Design a variety of endings, so you have endings that you love and new ones that bring a delightful surprise. Continue to innovate new compositions to enjoy your music of pleasure for the rest of your life.

How you build trust, create intimacy, and inspire her emotional experience are just as important! The trust factor is the key! That means that she genuinely trusts that you have her best interest at heart at all times. The book will provide the system to build trust and the techniques to arouse her pleasure throughout.

Note On Summaries: I provided chapter summaries for you to review the important points before you implement the system. You can skip the summaries on your first reading. When you are ready to perform a night in the Seven Night to Ecstasy system, review the summaries and the night you'll implement in detail so she and you have the best experience.

Chapter Summary

Chapter One ~ Introduction ~

The Unique Value and Erotic Pleasures This Book Will Give You and Your Lover

1.1 The What and the How
The pleasure promise and how will this book deliver it

This book demonstrates scientific research that shows women have more and stronger orgasms from anal sex. You need to use a pleasurable and caring method to arouse a woman's body and mind so she can experience her ultimate orgasms and sexuality, especially through anal stimulation. Communication and building trust with small steps of experience are critically **important**.

1.2 Why
The unmet need to provide a detailed, step-by-step system to painless anal pleasure.

The other books on the market do not provide a step-by-step guide on how to take it slow; therefore, this book was developed. If you go too fast, you'll hurt her, and she will not trust you. Most likely, she'll not want to try again or will be irritated by your requests.

1.3 For Whom

Erotic delight for women and couples.

For women who are interested or whose man is interested in having and enjoying anal sexuality; for men who are interested or have a woman who wants them to become knowledgeable about how to introduce her to anal sexuality; and for couples who want to expand their realms of passionate and erotic pleasure.

1.4 The Solution and Benefits

All the HOT rewards you will experience

The SEPOR Method and the 7 Nights to Ecstasy System. The woman in your life will experience amazing orgasms from anal play and anal sexuality. You'll give her new delights of pleasure all throughout the process. You and your partner will attain new heights of intimacy and passion.

1.5 The Difference

The pleasurable difference in the techniques this book deliver.

a. A different strategy that arouses the body to seduce the mind.

b. 82 illustrations to effectively communicate what to do and how to do it.

c. The best anal toys, my favorite lubes, and where to buy them with discounts.

d. Hygiene strategies.

e. System, unique anal play activities, advanced techniques not found in any other resource.

1.6 The Results Are In
Research shows women have more and stronger orgasms from anal sex.

Growing awareness of it's pleasure is increasing acceptance and engagement.

a. Research shows that from the women surveyed, of those that had anal sex, 94% orgasmed, while only 66% orgasm during vaginal intercourse.

b. Variety in sexual acts leads to more orgasms in both sexes.

c. Anal orgasms do happen, as stated by a variety of women and online articles.

d. Anal orgasms are powerful, with contractions stronger than vaginal orgasms.

e. Her anatomy enables her to have anal orgasms through the stimulation of her pudendal nerve, which connects to the clitoris, the clitoral legs, and indirect stimulation of her G-spot. Adding direct stimulation of her clitoris enhances her arousal response.

f. Engagement in anal sex is increasing. In a 1992 study, 20.4% of women 18 to 59 tried anal sex, and in a study conducted between 2011 to 2015, 33.2% of women 15 to 44 tried anal sex, and almost 40% of women 24 to 34 tried anal sex. More online magazines are reporting increasing engagement across the world.

g. The topic of anal is a popular search term, even more than cooking and the stock market. More women are searching for anal sex on porn sites as well.

h. Many popular magazines like Cosmopolitan, Shape, Glamour, Self, and Women's Health are covering the topic of anal sex and increasing awareness of its pleasure.

i. Female empowerment has improved the quality sex.

j. More people of faith are engaging in a variety of sexual acts, including anal sexuality.

k. Sales in anal sex toys are also increasing, and another indicator of more people engaging in anal sexuality.

l. YouTube content on anal sex is also exploding. A YouTube video on how-to anal sex hit 19 million hits in seven months.

m. Anal sex reaches other levels of soulful experience and releases of deep-rooted tension.

n. Her ultimate pleasure lies in arousing multiple erogenous zones, including anal stimulation. By stimulating multiple erogenous zones like her clitoris, G-spot, U-spot, A-spot, Cervix, P-spot, K-spot, perineal sponge, anus, her breasts, neck, lips, ass cheeks, and her emotions simultaneously, she'll have her *ultimate orgasms*.

Chapter One

For updates on the sexual science and research, join the mailing list at the bottom of my website.

Chapter Two
Arouse Her Mind, Body, and Soul

The SEPOR Method and The 7 Nights to Ecstasy

2.1 Satisfy Her Soul
So you can discover new pleasures with trust

So let's get started! I originally was going to call the book "Gem Pleasure" because throughout the book I refer to a woman's anal ring and the inside as her "gem." I used the term "gem" to signifies a beautiful and precious part of her body that can give her lots of sexual ecstasy. Along with the genital areas, the gem is connected to and interwoven with millions of delicately sensitive nerve endings, which can yield incredibly pleasurable sensations. A very cool beta reader of my book from the UK informed me of something I thought was hilarious. In England, the term "gem" is slang for a sex worker and for a white woman having sex with a black man with a large penis. So stating, "she's quite a gem!" would be a totally different meaning than in the US! LOL For the record, that is not the meaning I intended, as explained above. Also, it's a one-syllable word that's easier to write frequently throughout the book.

I digress, back to the content. To inspire her to be open to enjoying stimulation there, you are going to have to fall in love with pleasuring her inside and out physically, mentally, and emotionally. When you are pleasuring her, get lost in that moment like there is nothing else that exists and every ounce of your energy is united with hers. You are fully engulfed in giving her pleasure and making her feel incredible.

To stimulate her mind and soul, let's talk about intimacy. Although this is not a book on relationships, communication and intimacy are important when venturing into anal sexuality. Since gem sex is a very intimate experience, you and your partner should have good communication and a playful attitude toward trying new things in the bedroom. Make sure you know what makes her feel most cared for or loved by you. Find out her "must have" to feel cared for: Is it what you do for her and how you do those things? Is it the things you say and how you say them? Or is it the kinesthetic feeling she has when you hold each other? All three are important, but make sure you deliver well on her "must have" for receiving caring/love. This concept is taught by Anthony Robbins and is similar to the teachings in the book the Five Love Languages.

Do all three to make her feel beautiful, cared for, sexy, and appreciated. Ensure that your make her feel this way prior, during, and after every session. Especially do things, say things, and hold her in ways that makes feel comfortable, confident, and gorgeous about her body as you stimulate her new pleasure zone. There are many books on relationships, communication, and sexuality. Read them, and become a master at making her feel incredible, both physically and mentally. She will be much more receptive to sexual exploration and adventure when you have the knowledge to make sure that all her emotional needs are covered.

Additionally, to have her be open to anal exploration, she needs to trust that you have her best interest at heart and a proper process. She needs to feel comfortable with you and feel that she can trust you to listen to her if she says to slow down or stop due to discomfort for any reason and that you'll gladly listen. Building trust is crucial—just put yourself in her shoes. You need to let her know that it does not matter how long it takes because you are there to give her pleasure and enjoy each other's passion, not trying to get to an end goal.

Let her know that even if it takes weeks or months for her, it does not matter because you are there to enjoy the sensual and erotic experiences of the journey. When you release the pressure of time and build trust, she will feel more relaxed and savor the HOT stimulation of her body, enabling the process to flow well. If you get impatient, you'll go too fast and hurt her, and typically, that will be the end of the ride because it will be hard for her to trust you again. This experience is about flowing in the moment together and having her erotic energy and passion becoming one with yours. Make it your art to kiss her and her entire body with all your being. Take the time to kiss her deliciously and connect with her throughout every experience. Make it your passion to erotically seduce her mind, body, and soul.

2.2 Seduce Her Body
So her mind eagerly wants more ~ The SEPOR Method

Here is an overview of a typical situation: A woman usually does not want to try gem sex because she is afraid it will hurt, hygiene, heard a bad story, or other. Some women also factor in religion. Most of these reasons can be overcome by gradually demonstrating to her body the pleasure she can feel from light gem play. With the right intention of only wanting to pleasure her and the right technique, she will slowly enjoy more and more. She will learn the incredible pleasure she can receive from it. Research has shown that women who engage in gem sex enjoy easier, more, and stronger orgasms.

The SEPOR Method is about starting with something small, showing her pleasure, and giving her an explosive orgasm every time.

The SEPOR Method is as follows:

S - Stimulate — Stimulate her so as to arouse her senses, body, erogenous zones, and her personal zones of pleasure. Sensually and passionately get her in the mood.

E - Excite — Excite her body with a new experience of arousal. For example, first, you'll just massage her outer gem, and on another night, you'll lick her outer gem. Each time you'll introduce a small but exciting new experience of exploration.

P - Pleasure — Spend time pleasuring her with the new experience while also doing what she already enjoys (kissing, licking her breasts, cunnilingus, etc.). Indulge in enjoying the moment without a goal.

O - Orgasm   After thoroughly enjoying the new experience, add stimulation that you know will bring her to orgasm. Continue to perform the new experience while you make her orgasm with what you know she loves, so she associates lots of satisfaction with the new stimulation.

R - Reaffirm   Talk to her about the experience. Find out what she liked most, if there were things she did not like, and things you did not try that she would have liked.

Every night has something new, so talk to her about every experience. Ask about speed, places that felt good or not, angling of your fingers, toys, and you when you enter her. Communicate in the moment to adjust on the fly and afterward. You don't want to devote a lot of time to doing something not enjoyable. Look at her facial expressions and body reactions for signs on how to adjust. Communicate how much you enjoy it and how much she turns you on. Ask her feedback by asking her questions in a sexy manner.

The SEPOR Method makes every step of the process incredibly pleasurable for her. Though the O in the SEPOR Method stands for orgasm, do not focus solely on getting her to orgasm. Indulge in pleasuring her so she can feel all your passion, heart, and soul and how turned on you are from enjoying the arousal together. It's like the difference of when a woman is giving a blowjob because she is trying to make you cum as opposed to when she is doing it because she is loving every moment of it. It's a big difference! Right! So love what you do; it makes the act sexual art.

The general advice out there is to go slowly, but I will provide a sense of measurement. You'll have a guideline on what to do per night to go slowly with only pleasure. Some women will be able to go faster, and you may have a desire to do so. If she is totally new and scared of gem sex, stick to the Seven Nights to Ecstasy System, as it will provide a baseline minimum to make the process gratifying, and it will be fun to go through. If she wants you to go faster because she has done an activity before, then go to the next night's activities in the system, and see how she feels. Remember, if you go too fast and do too much, she might have an uncomfortable experience, and that will probably end the fun. Therefore, enjoy the process so she yearns for more every session.

2.3 Communication

Arousing her sexuality to new exciting heights: The 7 Nights to Ecstasy System

Other books and DVDs usually advise or show a woman starting anal play in a bent-over-on-all-fours position. This position is great once she has already started enjoying anal fondling and licking, but if she has never done any anal play, she should start on her back. Lubricants used on her gem will flow onto the bed, away from her vagina. In the beginning, on her back builds the most intimacy and provides easy communication. By starting with her on her back and doing everything you would do in the initiation of a sensual experience in missionary position, you'll build intimacy. You are about to engage in an act that is one of the most intimate in the sexual realm. It has provided a deep sense of connection for thousands of lovers. This position will enable you to look into each other's eyes, see her facial expressions, and gauge her comfort to make sure she is enjoying every moment.

If it is a new relationship, make sure to find out the things that arouse her so you can do them while simultaneously stimulating her gem. Does she like biting? How deep, how wide, and where? What kind of kisses does she like: sensual, passionate, or erotic? What type of play does she like? Soft and sensual, more intense and rough, or all of the above in the right sequence? Find this out by taking the lead to do the above and get feedback. You want to lead discovery in a sexy manner and always think of how you can do things differently to create novelty in your experiences. Asking her might be biased with how the previous person did those things, which could have been poorly, and different from how it will feel with you. Lead the discovery of her boundaries and creatively expand her sexual desires and delights.

As you progress through each night, see what turns her on, and how she likes things. Get specifics when engaging in the process on slower, faster, deeper, softer, or changing positions, etc. You want to become a Jedi Master at licking, kissing, sucking, biting, and pleasuring her entire body. Become a master of erotic talk before, during, and after sex sessions. Let her know how hot she is, how much she turns you on, how much you enjoy her body, how sexy she moves, how delicious she tastes, how much you enjoy the way she sounds, how good she feels (every part), and let her know what things turn you on.

Find out what type of language turns both of you on, and use it throughout your sessions. Talk about what specific words and statements turn both of you on so you can use the language that will have the most powerful effect. Again, take the lead introducing sex talk terms and phrases, and get feedback. When you push the envelope in sex talk, it frees her from feeling embarrassed. If she freely provides statements, then you are a lucky man. Statements will get more provocative and hotter as you progress through the system, so get feedback by Night Three, then again for Night Five, and again at Night Seven. Continue the dialogue in case you think of new things you want to hear and/or to discover new things she wants to hear. Express how you both want the statements said; the "how" matters as much as the "what."

2.4 The 7 Nights to Ecstasy System

The solution

Night 1 Excite and pleasure her by only massaging the outer gem with your finger while licking her clitoris and her vagina. You'll use the following pleasuring techniques, Finger Rolls, and Palm and Gem Pleasure (all techniques are explained in Chapter Three and suggested breaks in between nights are in last paragraph).

Night 2 Pleasure her by licking her outer gem, while playing with her clitoris and vagina. Lick her vagina and gem while using your fingers to provide simultaneous pleasure. Start with Night One techniques. Technique to use, Grooves For Her.

Night 3 Pleasure her by licking her clitoris and vagina, massaging her G-spot, inserting a finger in her gem. Pinky finger first, then your middle finger. Start with Night One and Two techniques. Techniques to use, Groves For Her Pump, and Palm and Curve Pleasure.

Night 4 Pleasure her with a beginner anal vibrating toy and two fingers while licking her clitoris and massaging her G-spot.

Implement techniques from Nights One, Two, and Three. Techniques to use, the importance of CT, and ooohOOOHs. Try to move on to Night Five within five nights of this night to maintain conditioning.

Night 5 Pleasure her with a gradually bigger girth toy and/or three fingers (not at same time) while licking her clitoris and massaging her G-spot. Implement techniques from Nights One, Two, Three, and Four. Technique to use, Pleasure Twists. This Night might need to be repeated with bigger toys closer to the girth of your size. Associate intimacy with anal play. Night Six should occur within six nights to maintain progress.

Night 6 Arouse her with activities from Nights One thru Five, then play with a toy on her clitoris. Techniques to use, Grooves For Her, Leave-In, Waves of Lubrication, My Vibe, Pleasure Twists, oooh OOOHs, the Gem Slide, MyVibe, and the Five Steps to Enter Her Gem. You'll insert yourself very slowly and sensually while using simultaneous stimulation to her outer gem, vagina, U-spot, and nipples. Start with missionary and slow sensual movements. The mentioned techniques are what will make the process smooth and pleasurable for her; read them in detail. Night Seven should occur within five nights.

Night 7 Arouse her with techniques from Nights One thru Six. Move on to deeper, faster movements and different positions; while having a toy on her clitoris, stimulate her vagina, G-spot, and other erogenous zones. Technique to use, Ride The Grooves.

The key is to make every new small step during each night an experience that pleasures her deeply. Each night has new pleasuring techniques to use which bring her to orgasm while stimulating her gem and leaves her yearning for more next time. You can do Nights One, Two, and Three consecutively. It would be good to take at least a one-night break between Nights Three and Four. You can take a longer break in between Nights Four and Five. I recommend no more than six nights because if you wait too long, you might lose some of the progress you've made to accustom her gem to the toy girth you last used. The break between nights six to seven can be one to four days. Once you have gone in her gem as long as her body is feeling good, you can try again. Always make sure she is feeling good 100 percent. Caring and patience is the key enabling her to love it and crave it.

How to build trust when introducing anal play.

Even though you two might trust each other in other aspects of your relationship, it is imperative to build her trust in you, your skills, and your intentions in this aspect—don't just assume she will trust you. An important factor of the Seven Nights to Ecstasy System is that you are going to build trust with her every night by consistently delivering on your word. Promise her that you will:

Go slow and only do the activity of each night.

Immediately stop if something is uncomfortable to her.

Listen to her feelings and sensations so you can adjust accordingly.

If you do the above, as the nights progress, her trust will build; **she will relax and enjoy because you have delivered on your word every time.** How you build trust with her will determine how far you get in this journey of sexual bliss.

2.5 Assess How She Feels About Anal Play
How to introduce and design the process for her, The Three Night Delight System and The Custom System

Tell her that you want to satisfy all of her sexual desires and fantasies. It is your passion to give her pleasure and to excite all of her senses. Ask her, is there something she would like to experience because you would enjoy making her fantasy come to life? Ask her what kind of activities she likes. Ask about sex in different locations, positions, toys, hair pulling, spanking, biting, a hand sensually holding her neck, and gem play. Ask about a variety of sensual activities before you ask about gem play. After each question, if she says she has not tried something, ask her if she has ever been curious or interested in trying that activity. Use the above system to cover a variety of sexual activities so the conversation naturally flows when you get to the gem play question. The following are solutions to three scenarios based on her answer.

Her Ultimate Pleasure

Scenario One

She says that she has never tried gem sex or play, that she is scared of it from bad stories she's heard, or has never been interested for a wide variety of reasons. This is the scenario that typically happens, and it is one of the main reasons I wrote this book. Women can be scared for many reasons, possible pain, not being clean, or the guy is too big, etc. Also, people women do not know the latest research and the science on the pleasure anal stimulation provides. If she says no to gem play, ask her why so you know what her concerns are. That way, you'll know how to address this topic with her.

Most guys think they can talk a woman into doing it and follow the typical advice out there (have her relax, go slow, and use lots of lube). That is NOT going to work. Women would never have a bad experience if that worked, but they still do! Many tried it because they were open to experiencing something new. However, they did not do it again because the man did not know how to introduce it, which led to an uncomfortable experience from bad advice.

This is a sad situation because women CAN have more and stronger orgasms! It just takes the right process and intention. One key reason this content works to introduce anal sexuality is because of its intention philosophy. **Your intention should NOT be to get her to have anal sex; you have to throw away self-motivated plans. The only way it works is if you genuinely enter this journey with the sole purpose of MAKING HER FEEL INCREDIBLE.**

Yes, it is all about loving to indulge in her ecstasy and pleasuring her in many ways. Anal stimulation is just one of the ways you want to be able to include the variety you give her. Since her pleasure is the goal, even at the slightest hint of discomfort, you stop or adjust so it is always good for her. With this intention, you build trust with her, which is a crucial factor in having her enjoy this new stimulation.

Most of the advice out there assumes that you can have anal sex in one night with a woman who has never done it before. Not for most women! Just put yourself in her shoes; you would not want to feel rushed. That might make you scared or nervous. This system is designed to seduce her body with small exciting steps of pleasure, letting her enjoy every step of the way so she yearns eagerly for the next step.

Commit to reading this book thoroughly; do not skip steps or go fast through them. Perform the detailed instructions to make it good for her. Sincerely promise her that you are only going to go as far as she is comfortable and enjoying the process. Even if it takes longer for your partner than the Seven Nights to Ecstasy System because of her personal evolution, just flow in those moments of hot sexuality. If all your energy and soul is engulfed in every kiss, lick, suck, and caress with no pressure, you'll gradually progress further and further. Through flowing together and unselfish intentions, she will experience immense fulfillment from anal sexuality.

Here is an approach that you can take for Scenario One. Implement the communication and actions to make her feel cared for, appreciated, and sexy. Perform Night One stimulation; since it is nonpenetrative, you'll only arouse around and on top of her gem. Communicate exactly what you'll do in the moment; follow the instructions and see how she likes the stimulation you are giving her. Only implement a night if you have enough time to make it really good for her. If she likes it, then implement Night Two, it is also nonpenetrative. Only move forward to the next night if you see that she's enjoying the stimulation.

Get feedback to make sure she is. If she feels like you are going too fast, then repeat the activities that she does savor. Now that you have aroused her to like some anal stimulation without any penetration, ask her how it felt. If she responds positively, you can introduce this book to her so she can read the pleasure she will experience, and so she can clean accordingly for the upcoming nights. She can now look forward to the process and know what arousal activities and stimulation to expect.

If she is still a little hesitant, do the stimulation from Nights One and Two again with even more passion using the Grooves For Her Technique. Stay doing what she responds to until she is yearning to experience a little more. It might take longer—that is okay. Your objective is not to get to the end quickly; it's to indulge in having her enjoy the stimulation. She needs to feel that there's no rush.

When she is ready for more, Implement Night Three; perform the hygiene activities for this night and the following nights. After each night, ask what she liked and what she might want you to modify. Continue to excite her senses and strengthen your connection. She then will yearn for more and more. Keep progressing until you complete the Seven Nights

If it takes longer for your partner to go through the system, that is fine, weeks or more. It does not matter how long it takes for your specific situation because it's about the new arousal you two are experiencing. Your mission is to create gratifying moments together. You'll go only as far as she continues to enjoy it, so the responsibility is on you to make her feel phenomenal!

Scenario Two

If she states that she never tried it but is interested, she can read the book first so she knows what will happen. This book is designed to seduce the mind of a female reader so she is inspired to try the pleasure of anal sexuality, but it is written addressing the man because he is going to implement the instructions. The book is structured to stimulate a woman through what she reads and sees in the Seven Nights to Ecstasy System and the Advanced chapter. I added art to the instructional images to elicit more visual stimulation and progressively arouse her imagination through the sexual fantasy ahead of time.

Therefore, after a woman reads the book, the goal is for her to say, "I want experience my ultimate orgasms with you!" She'll learn that she will enjoy stimulation to her clitoris, G-spot, U-spot, vagina, perineal sponge, her gem, and other erogenous zones simultaneously. When a woman experiences this arousal in concert with your passion and connection, this leads her to have explosive, full-body orgasms.

It is optimal if she reads it in a sensual environment, for example, in bed with sexy music playing. Free erotic music playlists available at YouTube.com/EroticFlow. Then you can read it and discuss it together afterward. Also, you two can read this book together so you two can talk about it as you read it. If you read it together, the man can read it to his woman, and whenever I state "you'll," he could read out loud "I'll" and lead her through a fantasy. She will know that you have spent the time to make sure that she has a hot experience throughout. Implement the Seven Nights to Ecstasy System with the advice I provided in scenario one.

Ladies, if you bought the book and are introducing the topic, let your partner know that you read an article that women can have more and stronger orgasms from anal stimulation. And, you want to experience that with him. If you two have the time to read it together do as instructed above. If not, have him read Content Insights, Sections 1.3, 1.4, 1.6, and the rest of the book. Then, decide which system you will use the 7 Nights, 3 Nights or Custom, explained in Scenario Three. If he is not interested in anal sex, have him read Sections 1.3, 1.4, 1.6, Chapter 2, and 4 and scan the rest of the book.

Chapter Two

After, restate that you want to have your most fulfilling and hot sex with him. If he is still hesitant ask him what is he willing to try and start from there.

Scenario Three

If she states that she has tried gem play before, then ask what she did and how long it has been. Also, whether she had a positive or negative experience. For example, do you enjoy having your gem licked? Or how about a finger in your gem while your clitoris is licked? Or used anal toys? If she has done any gem play before, then assess **Option One**, the **Three-Night Delight System** which is for more advanced couples that have experience with anal play. Assess what she has done to see if this is a better solution for you.

The **3-Night Delight System** is as follows - **Use SEPOR every night**:

Night 1   Excite her with the activities of the Nights 1, 2, and 3 from the 7 Night System.

Night 2   Start by stimulating her with the activities that she loves from the first three nights. Then use the techniques from Nights 4 and 5. Use the dilation system to the size close to your girth. Remember simultaneous stimulation of multiple spots.

Night 3   Arouse her with the techniques from Nights One thru Five. Then, use the techniques from Nights 6 and 7. Make sure you use the Five Steps to Enter Her Gem (covered in Night Six). Since this will be the first time you are entering her gem with your penis, be conscious of not going too long. You don't want her to be sore. So do it for as long as it is feeling really good to her. Ask her to tell you if she experiences any discomfort at the first sign of any discomfort, and pause until she is comfortable. If the discomfort continues, even slightly, use the exit technique described in Night Six. Then use her favorite stimulation to bring her to orgasm. If on Night Three she still needs more time, let her know it is ok and it does not matter how long it takes; it is about the pleasure you two are experiencing.

Option Two is the **Custom System**; if options one or two do not seem to provide the best solution because she has a lot of gem play experience but wants to make sure it is good for her with you, then implement all the pleasuring techniques from the Seven Nights System in a single session until you reach what she has done before. Spend time delighting her with what she has already done and continue from that point forward using the remaining night-by-night system. The Custom System can be as short as one or two nights for a woman that has anal play experience with thicker toys close to your girth.

IMPORTANT NOTE FOR A ONE NIGHT ATTEMPT: The only time you should do it in one night is in the following two situations. First, if she uses anal toys that are really close to the size of your girth frequently. Second, if she has had anal sex before with a girth close to yours, enjoyed it, had it multiple times, and not more than three months in the past. If it was a long time ago, consider you have to accustom her body for anal sex. For either of the cases above, follow the instructions of Night Six. Though, if neither is the case, or she has not had a girth close to yours, it is better to add nights so you can build trust and pleasure.

Before each night of the Seven Nights to Ecstasy System or a custom system, reread the activities for that night so the instructions are fresh in your mind or both of your minds.

For the ladies that bought this book on their own, if you are interested but your man is not for a variety of reasons, I met some men who felt like this. What changed their mind was finding out that science now proves that he could give you your most incredible orgasms and more of them! And he wanted to be the one to do that for his woman.

For men that are not interested and your wife or girlfriend gave you the book to read, I'm sure you want to be the lover to make her feel her ultimate pleasure. If she has never experienced it, you'll stand out as the lover that was able to satisfy her like that. If she enjoyed anal stimulation before, then she is probably fantasizing about it! If you do not provide that satisfaction, she might imagine having this treat with someone else or reminisce enjoying it with someone prior. You don't want that! Be her best lover.

2.6 Seduction Philosphy

In summary, the strategy to get her from curiosity to sexual fulfillment—or from NO WAY to Oh My God, that was AMAZING—is to arouse her body and her mind simultaneously, lead with pleasure. Doing small things that feel good that stimulate and tease her senses. This is better and sexier than logically trying to convince her verbally. The intention is always about having her feel incredible, flowing in the moment together, and NOT about getting to a goal.

2.7 Patience is Pleasure

The Seven Nights System is a baseline in terms of the amount of time you should take. If she needs longer, then take longer; no matter how long it takes, weeks or months, it is worth your patience. The process will be enjoyable and erotic for both of you. It is multiple nights of incredible pleasure that lead to immense ecstasy! The length of time enables you to build trust. There is no need for her to worry about pain or going too fast; it is not about jumping into the deep end of the pool quickly because the only thing she will do on Night One is touch the water with her pinky toe at the shallow end.

If she wants to hold back and only go as far as the activities of a certain Night, then just keep doing that step so good she loves it! Do that activity with all your passion for as many nights as she wants. Let her know you get off on her happiness and by doing that step alone.

Over time, if you stimulate and tease her deliciously, you'll inspire her desire, and she'll pull you to experience more. Let her pleasure pull you, don't push. Then, you can progress to the next small step. If you become too eager and go too fast, the ride will be over! She and you will miss out on amazing experiences. So enjoy the ride!

2.8 Set-up Ahead of Time to Be Smooth During

As you progress through the steps, have all your tools and toys ready. I cover cleaning, toys, and lubes in Chapter Four. I cover them later because even though the instructions are written for a man to implement, this book is designed to arouse a female reader, so I put the more stimulating content first.

When using lubes and toys, you want to smoothly progress through the stimulation instead of having to take breaks to get the lubricant and all of the toys. Keep a cool-looking box or bag for these items beside your bed, allowing you to easily reach them when you need them. At each night of the process, you'll need different toys. Plan accordingly to have them clean, charged, and set them up for easy access and cool display.

Have at least two bottles of lubricant in case you can't locate the bottle during the action; don't break the vibe, have a backup. Why do you need a cool box or bag for your toys? Because presentation is important. It is just like how guys like it when girls wear lingerie—the wrapping adds to the arousal and interest. Cut and file your fingernails so that there are no sharp edges. Cleanse each other and check yourselves right before sex; ensure you both smell and taste good.

Music is important to set the right vibe and inspire a sensual flow. Go to EroticFlow.com/HUPVideos to hear an audio recording on **The Importance of Music** and view a video on **flowing with the music** you select. Set-up your playlist or channel to ignite the moment. I provide several music playlists for you to enjoy at YouTube.com/EroticFlow.

Chapter Summary

Chapter Two ~ Arouse Her Mind, Body, and Soul
The SEPOR Method and The 7 Nights to Ecstasy

2.1 Satisfy Her Soul ~
So you can discover new pleasures with trust

a. Her "gem" is the beautiful part of her that you'll be playing with and entering.

b. Build intimacy, caring, flirtation, passion, and trust outside the bedroom so things can flow inside the bedroom.

c. Find out her "must haves" in terms of how she receives and expresses caring/love.

d. Become a master of kissing her everywhere and in a variety of ways that turn her on. Kiss her with all your soul to connect with her deeply. Make sure you take the time to kiss her deliciously and connect with her throughout the entire journey.

e. Building trust is imperative!

2.2 Seduce Her Body
So her mind eagerly wants more ~ The SEPOR Method

a. You are going to take only small steps to give her lots of pleasure so she eagerly wants a little more.

b. The SEPOR Method

S = **Stimulate** her senses and body the way she likes.

E = **Excite** her body with the new experience of arousal, a new small step of pleasure.

P = **Pleasure,** spend time indulging in pleasuring her with the new experience combined with other things she already enjoys.

O = **Orgasm,** after thoroughly pleasuring her with the new experience, combine it with what you know will give her a good orgasm, so she will associate the new experience with lots of pleasure.

R = **Reaffirm,** talk to her about the experience and find out what she liked, what you could have done differently, or if there was something she did not like. Let her know how much she turns you on and how beautiful she is, inside and out.

2.3 Communication
Arousing her sexuality to new exciting heights and the 7 Nights to Ecstasy System

a. Become a master of her intimate pleasures by communicating with her to find out exactly what drives her wild.

b. Let her know what you like to make her a master of your pleasures.

2.4 The 7 Nights to Ecstasy System ~
The solution

Use the SEPOR Method on every night.

Night 1   Pleasure her by only massaging the outer gem with your finger while licking her clitoris and her vagina. Techniques, Finger Rolls, and Palm and Gem Pleasure.

Night 2   Pleasure her by licking her outer gem while playing with her clitoris and vagina. Lick her vagina and gem while using your fingers to provide simultaneous pleasure. Technique, Grooves For Her. Start with Night One techniques.

Night 3   Pleasure her by licking her clitoris and vagina, massaging her G-spot, and inserting a finger in her gem. Start with a pinky finger, then progress to your middle finger.

Chapter Two

Start with Night One and Two techniques. Techniques, Finger Rolls, and Palm and Gem Pleasure.

Night 4 Pleasure her with a beginner gem vibrating toy and two fingers (not at the same time) while licking her clitoris and massaging her G-spot. Techniques, the importance of CT, and ooohOOOHs. Implement techniques one, two, and three. Try to move on to Night Five within five nights to maintain conditioning.

Night 5 Pleasure her with a gradually bigger girth toy or three fingers while licking her clitoris and massaging her G-spot. Implement techniques one, two, three, and four. Technique, Pleasure Twists. Depending on the size of the guy, this Night might need to be repeated with another bigger toy closer to the girth of the guy. Try moving to Night Six within five nights.

Night 6 Warm her up with activities from Nights One thru Five, then play with a toy on her clitoris. Techniques, the Grooves For Her, Leave-In, Waves of Lubrication, My Vibe, Pleasure Twists, oooh OOOHs, The Gem Slide, My Vibe, and the Five Steps to Enter Her Gem. Insert yourself very slowly and sensually while using simultaneous stimulation to her outer gem, vagina, U-spot, and nipples. Start with missionary and slow sensual movements. Try moving to Night Seven within five nights.

Night 7 Warm her up with activities from Nights One thru Six. Move on to deeper, faster, movements, and different positions while having a toy on her clitoris. Make sure you stimulate her vagina, G-spot, U-spot, and other erogenous zones. Technique, Ride The Grooves. Delight her with the Chapter Five anal play and position techniques and sex that gives her explosive orgasms. Continue to explore advanced play.

Introduce gem play by building trust. Only do small steps to give her a pleasurable experience and deliver on your word every night.

Nights 4 to 7 should preferably have at least a one-night break in between.

Start with your partner on her back to see her facial expressions easily, communicate easily, and build the most intimacy possible for the journey into anal ecstasy. Designate a hand for anal massage and the other hand for vagina and clitoral massage.

2.5. Assess How She Feels About Anal Play
Introduce and design the process for her, 3 Night Delight System, and Custom

Talk about what she has done before in her sexual experimentation. Out of the experiences she has never tried, ask her if she has ever been interested in experiencing them, including gem play. Find out her fantasies and new things she wants to try. Then make them happen for her and you. If she says no to gem play, ask her why, so you know what her concerns are. That way, you'll know how to address this topic with her. You are only going to take small steps pleasuring her and only go as far as she likes and never go further than what she is enjoying. The key is that you are going to master pleasuring her so thoroughly that she will gradually want more and more.

Depending on her anal sex experience and sentiment toward anal sex, you'll implement the instructions for scenarios one, two, or three.

Decide whether to use the Seven Night, Three Night, or Customer System to introduce her to gem sex.

IMPORTANT NOTE FOR A ONE-NIGHT ATTEMPT: The only time you should do it in one night is in the following two situations. First, if she uses toys that are really close to the size of your girth frequently in her gem. Second, if she has had anal sex before with a girth close to yours, enjoyed it, then she knows she will have a good experience. Still consider your girth. If you know you are above average, go slower to make sure she is good with your shape. For either of the cases above, follow the instructions of Night Six. If neither are the case, it is better to add nights so you can build trust and pleasure.

2.6 Seduction Philosophy

a. The strategy to lead her from curiosity to fulfillment, or from NO to Oh My God that was AMAZING, is to arouse her body and mind simultaneously; lead with pleasure in small steps.

2.7 Patience is Pleasure

a. The 7 Nights to Ecstasy is a baseline measurement. Depending on your size and her anatomy, it may take longer. No matter how long it takes, it's all good, enjoy the process.

b. In the seven nights, you're only going to go as far as she feels good. Continue to pleasure her with the activities she likes to do and that make her feel incredible. If you do these things for as long as she likes, she'll start to enjoy a little bit more. It's scientifically proven women have easier, more, and stronger orgasms from gem play and gem sex.

c. REMEMBER: IF YOU GO TOO FAST AND GET TOO EAGER, YOU MIGHT END UP HURTING HER. IF THE TRUST IS GONE, THE RIDE WILL PROBABLY BE OVER! SO TAKE THE TIME TO ENJOY THE RIDE!

2.8 Set-up Ahead of Time to Be Smooth During

a. As you progress through the steps, you'll need toys and lubes. Instead of going back and forth into drawers and closets, have all your tools of the trade set up ahead of time.

b. Presentation is important. Get a cool box or bag that you can easily access. Keep it next to you when you are performing pleasuring activities. Keep two bottles of lube next to you in case you can't locate one.

c. Cut and file your fingernails so that there are no sharp edges. Cleanse each other and check yourselves right before sex; ensure you both smell and taste good.

Chapter Three
7 Nights to Ecstasy

The Process of Pleasuring Her and Giving Her Thrilling Ogasms Every Step of the Way to Anal Ecstasy

3.1 The Process in Detail
How to perform every touch, lick, and caress

In this chapter, I'll cover the seven nights in detail. The amount of detail serves two purposes. The first is to let you know exactly what to do. You can add your own flavor to the process. The second is to demonstrate to the woman in your life the pleasure she'll experience throughout the process. Ladies, when you read the content, imagine your man doing all the activities to you. If you are going to enjoy the process with a woman or on your own, great! Advice on these topics was recently requested, therefore, I added content to address both in the Resources section. You'll have amazing pleasure and orgasms with a man, a woman, or on your own. Men, visualize yourself doing the activities; it will help you remember the steps and techniques.

Read Chapter Four before engaging in any gem play; there are important rules to follow in terms of hygiene. Remember to view every night as an opportunity to create sexual art together, both physically and emotionally. Stop at the designated points so you can tease her body to yearn for more next time. **It's not about rushing her into it but loving her into it.** So let's start. Bold underlined technique names are videos on the book website.

Chapter Three

3.2 Night 1
Beginning a new world of pleasure

After implementing the communication advice from Chapter Two, select your system and begin Night One. Have her lay on her back. Kiss, lick, and caress her lips, neck, shoulders, breasts, nipples, stomach, pelvic area, thighs, and all of her unique erogenous zones. As you are kissing her, start lightly playing with her clitoris and her vagina with your fingers. Have her spread her legs wide so you have access to her gem. Here, you are going to move from kissing her lips to her breasts and her stomach while simultaneously caressing her clitoris and vaginal lips lightly [See Figure 3.1].

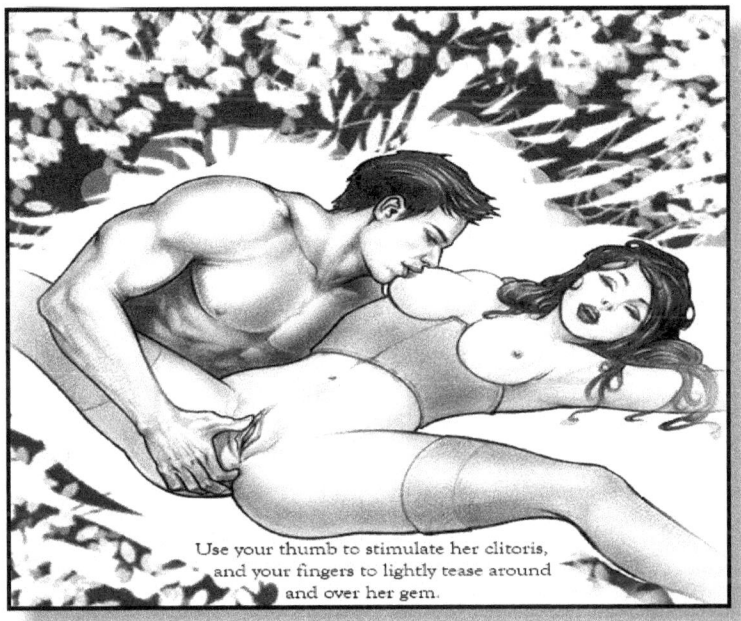

Figure 3.1

You want to spend time getting her really wet in this manner. Slowly dip the tip of your finger in her vagina to let more wetness out. As your finger starts to get wetter, go in a little deeper and put slight pressure downward to massage the bottom of her vagina, her perineal sponge. The downward massage will stimulate her and induce more wetness to come out so you can guide it down to her tang (the area in between her vagina and gem). Spread the wetness around her tang with your fingers while caressing her

Her Ultimate Pleasure

Figure 3.2

clitoris with your thumb. See how she reacts to you going up and down from her vagina to her tang [See Figure 3.2]. Most women will enjoy this. Tease around her gem about an inch and a half away from her gem for a while to build arousal. Tell her in a hot sexual manner that you want to massage around and over her gem to see how she enjoys a caress on top and that you have no intention of inserting your fingers in her gem. You just want to caress her entire body to see how she likes it.

Have your fingers take longer strokes up and down, making sure your thumb continues to caress her clitoris and vagina at the same time you are kissing her lips and breasts. Bring her wetness to the area around her gem. Lightly caress your middle finger over her gem and kiss her passionately; come back up to circle her vagina. You don't want to focus too much on her gem in the beginning; you just want to arouse around it and tease it.

Alternate the pleasure between where she is comfortable and the new area of exploration. This method does not involve any surprise moves. Then go back down and start to caress around her gem with circular motions.

Now stimulate the outside of her gem and over the center of her gem, but no penetration. Have her enjoy the stimulation of the area while lost in your kisses and the arousal of her other hot spots. Get her gem very wet with her juices, and as you continue to play with her clitoris, put a portion of your thumb in her vagina as your fingers play with her gem [**See Figure 3.3**]. You can put a little more sensual pressure on the gem to tease it, but do NOT try to go in; remember, build trust. Do this for a while so she can get used to the caressing of her clitoris, vaginal lips, tang, and gem.

Another stimulation technique is called the **Finger Rolls.** Pour lube on your fingers and lubricate her clitoris and gem generously, position your hand like

Chapter Three

Figure 3.3

in the previous Figure 3.2 with your thumb on her clitoris, and massage her clitoris while placing your little finger at the bottom of her gem. Then, slide your little finger up across her gem; follow it with your ring finger, middle finger, and first finger. Roll all fingers slowly and sensually while applying a little pressure. Speed up a little and change the direction of the roll. Do all this while you are playing with her clitoris with your thumb. Your other hand can be playing with her nipples while you suck her nipples as well. Lube tends to be cool in temperature, so it is good practice to first pour it on your fingers and then lubricate her so the lube warms up.

The next stimulation technique is the **Palm and Gem Pleasure.** Lubricate her clitoris and lips generously so the lubrication extends to the size of your palm. Place the top of your palm on her clitoris, and then sensuously massage her gem and all around it with your first finger. Your middle finger massages her tang, and your ring finger goes inside of her vagina to massage her G-spot. Massage her clitoris with your palm by moving it in a circular motion, up and down and side to side, while using your first finger to play with her gem. Your middle and ring finger play inside and outside her vagina **[See Figure 3.4]**. Also, do finger rolls on her gem, vagina, and clitoris.

IMPORTANT: While having sex, sensually massage around and over her gem using the finger play techniques explained for this night. Use all parts of your hand, both front and back of fingers, to provide variety. Imagine sending warm energy to your palm and fingers while you massage her gem area. You can do so in missionary, doggy style, on her side, and a variety of positions.

Review positions like the E3, V-Spot Massage, and Missionary Work activities in Chapter Five, but DO NOT try to go inside her gem with your fingers. Just stimulate the outside for now. If she has not had this type of anal play before, then let this be it for Night One. You're providing stimulation and building trust. Give her a great orgasm during sex and include the gem play described above so she associates lots of pleasure to gem play as she orgasms. If she enjoyed the experience, then you can move on to Night Two.

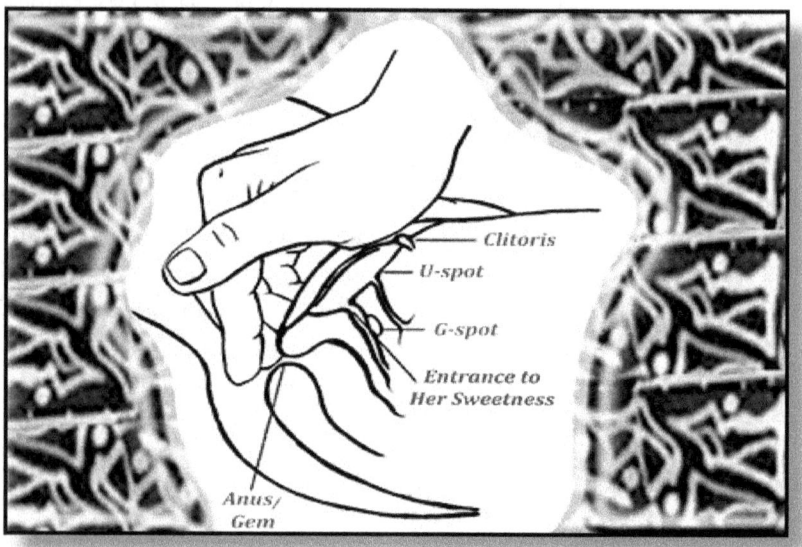

Figure 3.4

3.3 Night 2
Feel the warmth of my passion

On this night, you are going to use erotic cunnilingus and finger play to stimulate her while simultaneously arousing her gem. Take a shower together; sensually clean the outside of her gem. She or you should apply a little bit of soap on her gem with a little finger so the soap goes slightly inside her gem since you'll be licking her. You want to make sure the hygiene factor is good/clean. Or have her clean well on her own.

When you get to the bed, place her on her back; she'll feel a deeper sense of connection, intimacy, and comfort than in doggy style position. Also, you can better gauge her facial expressions and reactions as you start engaging in stimulating her gem from this position. Also, make eye contact with her to let her know that her scent is mouthwatering, that she tastes delicious, and that you love her body.

After doing all the foreplay of Night One, put her legs in the air, start kissing and licking from her feet or ankles and work your way down to her

Chapter Three

Figure 3.5

calves in circular motions. Go on to her thighs, lick, kiss, and take deep sensuous bites of her inner thigh, then sensually kiss, lick and bite further down. As you get to her vagina, slow down. Sensually lick on the outside of her vagina and all around the area between her lips and legs. Take deep, soft, sensuous bites into that area [See Figure 3.5].

Then, start near her leg and begin to glaze her vagina with the wetness of your tongue. Move across her vagina very lightly so she can feel the warmth of your breath and lightly feel the warm wetness of your tongue as you go across to the other side. Take the same sensuous, soft, deep bites on the other side and come back to glaze across again. This time, let her feel more of your tongue.

Lightly massage her gem with your fingers. Circle your tongue around her clitoris and suck it, massage her clitoris with your lips and tongue while sucking it. As you suck her clitoris massage by moving your tongue in a come here motion, side to side, up and down, and in circles. Make out with her clitoris. As you lick her wetness, have your fingers mirror

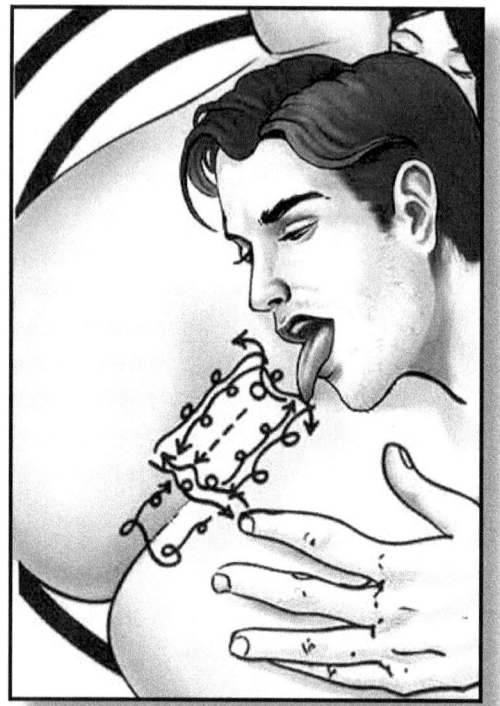

Figure 3.6

your tongue stroke. Glide your tongue across her lips several more times, each time with more passion. Direct all your energy to your mouth, lips, and tongue. Treat her wetness like it is your favorite dessert in the world. Let her wetness drip from your tongue onto her clitoris and lips.

Start taking longer licks down toward her gem. First, just go down to her tang. Stimulate every inch of her tang, tease, and come back up. Let her enjoy the teasing and pleasure on her tang for a bit. Start massaging her clitoris lightly with your fingers. Have her enjoy the simultaneous stimulation of you licking her tang and playing with her clitoris [See Figure 3.6]. Stay there for several seconds and come back up to lick her vagina again while still playing with her clitoris. Do this several times to arouse the area and increase her excitement. With hot sexual talk, let her know how amazing she tastes.

Caress around her gem area with your fingers, just pleasuring around her gem area. Then tease her gem by very lightly crossing your wet finger across her gem once. Lick her lips passionately. Come down with your tongue around her gem. Lightly glide your tongue across her gem and go back to her lips. As you go back up this time, turn your head to the side, and from the bottom of her vagina, put both of her lips inside your lips and your tongue in between her lips. Suck upwards with both of her lips in your mouth to her clitoris. Suck, lick, and kiss her clitoris at the top. Do all of the above while sensuously caressing across her gem with your fingers.

Each time you go back down to her gem area, make sure your tongue is really wet and continue to arouse her lips and clitoris with your fingers.

Chapter Three

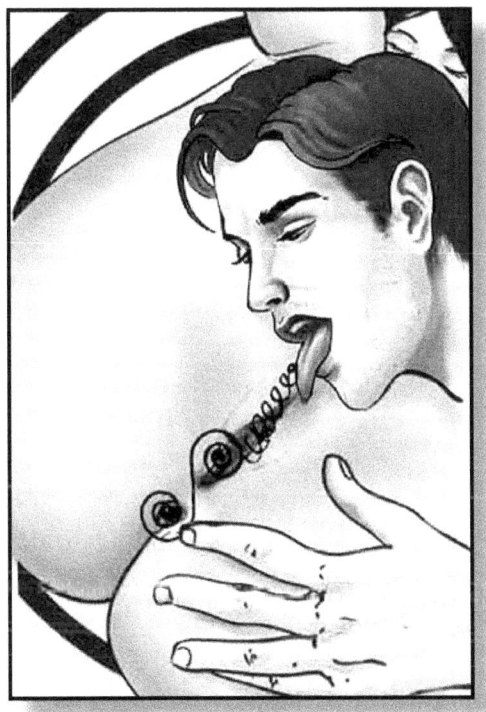

Figure 3.7

Gauge her pleasure and comfort level the closer you get. Her gem has many nerve endings that make stimulation of this area very pleasurable.

Have your finger follow your tongue around her gem. Start circling your tongue closer to her gem. Go back up to lick and indulge in her vagina, and then go back down, always caressing her clitoris [See **Figure 3.7**]. Let out the warmth of your breath as you pass over her gem while your lips are lightly circling it. The warmth of your breath and tongue is going to feel good to her. Lick the fingers on your free hand, then play with her nipples.

IMPORTANT: At this point, use a technique I call **Grooves For Her**. Bend your four fingers so that the tips of your fingers are touching the top of your palm, your thumb is against your first finger, and your palm is open [See **Figure 3.8**].

Use the middle row of your knuckles and thumb to massage up and down from her vagina to her gem. Lick your knuckles and slide them lightly from above her clitoris down past her gem on the first pass. Lick, suck, and kiss her clitoris while you sensually slide the grooves of your knuckles from the middle of her vagina down below her gem and up and down. The grooves of your knuckles will arouse her. Slowly increase pressure; the more pressure, the more the grooves provide stimulation. Put lube on her or your knuckles, and it will enable your knuckles to slip and slide up and down easily. Lick your fingers on your other hand and play with her nipples. Also, move your knuckles side to side and from different angles. Swirl your knuckles together in a circular motion and fan your knuckles, spacing them out separately in a circular motion. Ask her which feels best. **Succulently lick her clitoris and play with it using your**

Her Ultimate Pleasure

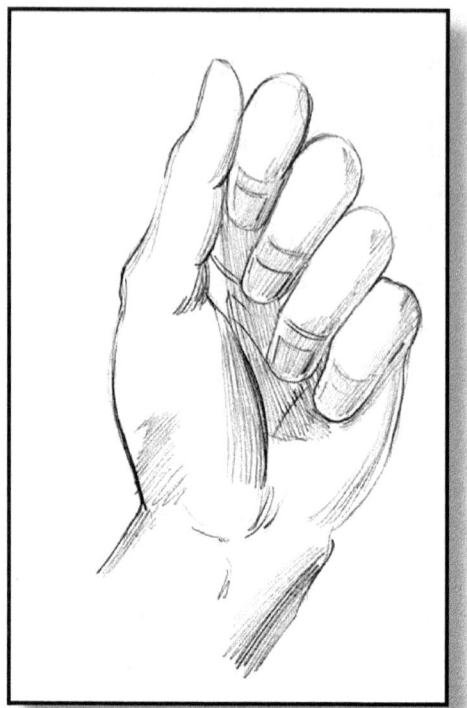

Figure 3.8

other hand throughout. **Make sure you do this technique!**

Now, you are pleasuring multiple erogenous zones: her nipples, clitoris, lips, and gem. She'll associate lots of gratification to the experience and not feel like you are only focusing on her gem.

Once you have aroused her with Grooves For Her, lick down to her tang and come back to her clitoris, then come down further and lick around her gem ring sensuously. Let her feel all your soul in every lick. Go back up to the vagina and kiss it softly, then more passionately, as though you were making out with her. Moan and pack as much emotion into the kiss as you can. It should feel as though that intense emotion is coming from your heart and traveling up to your lips. Become one with every lick. The high emotion enhances the intimate experience, and scientific research states that it creates higher vibration in your body. With your lips closed, moan and place your finger along the length of your lips, you'll feel the vibration. The vibration from your moans and emotion intensity will provide her more pleasure.

Write with your tongue in cursive on her clitoris, her vagina, her tang, and around her gem. Spell out how gorgeous she is, hot sex talk, and tell her out loud what you are writing. Gather as much of her juices as possible and write with your lips, tongue, breath, kisses, and while sucking [**See Figure 3.8.5**].

Apply a little more pressure on her gem with your tongue than previously. The softness and warmth of your tongue on her gem will feel good if you lick her sensually and with lots of emotion. Pull back, let the wetness of your tongue drip a little onto her gem, and lick it a little deeper. Tease her gem, go back up to lick her lips and clitoris. When you come back to her gem, use the middle finger of your left hand to play around her

Chapter Three

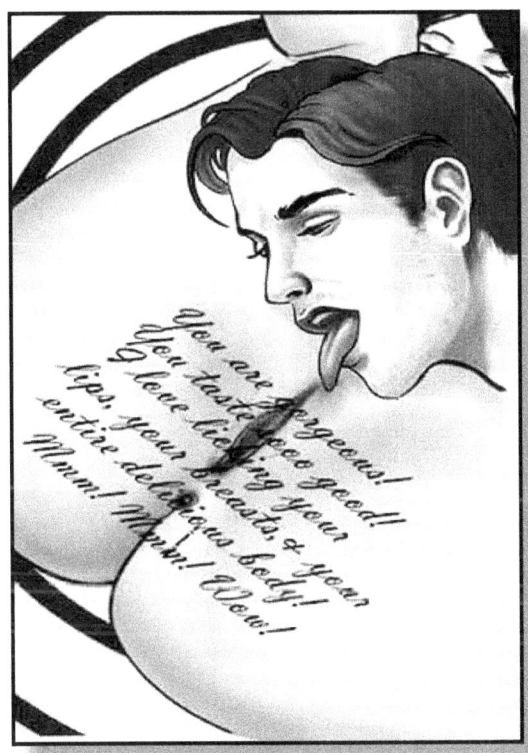

Figure 3.8.5

vagina. Then slowly insert your middle finger into her vagina. Have her move her legs back as far as possible to expose her gem more for you. If her legs don't move back very far because of limited flexibility, then try putting a pillow under her ass to angle her gem higher; this will give you better access for licking her gem while you play with her vagina and clitoris [See Figure 3.9].

Now use both hands to stimulate her vagina and clitoris while you lick her gem. Bring your left hand back down to caress the area around her gem and on her gem. Sensually play with her vagina and tang. Then, insert your first and/

Arouse her clitoris and gem.

Figure 3.9

or middle fingers into her vagina. Massage the inner areas of her vagina and perineal sponge while your right-hand plays with her clitoris. Circle your tongue in the middle of the gem. Begin to push your tongue lightly into the gem and lick around [See Figure 3.10].

Ask her if the stimulation feels good. If she is enjoying it, try to go deeper into her gem with your tongue. Muster as much passion as possible into every insertion of your tongue so she feels not only the physical pleasure but a strong connection with you. Ask her to spread her ass cheeks with her hands for you. Indulge in the play for as long as you would like her going

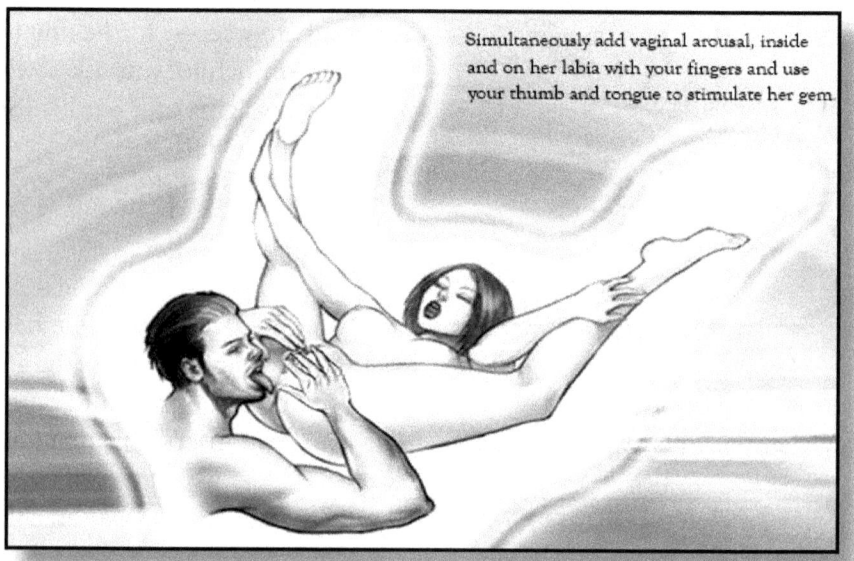

Figure 3.10

down on you, and longer. Squeeze and jiggle her ass cheek. Lick her gem and play with her breasts, nipples, and clitoris until she orgasms. Let this be Night Two. The process is to give her pleasure and orgasms at every step. You want to leave her wanting more, fantasizing about how good it felt, yearning for more gem stimulation, and eager to continue to play next time [See Figure 3.11].

Continue to have sex, play with her gem with your fingers and tongue with the techniques above throughout. As you are having sex, pull out and lick her vagina and gem. She is now accustomed to this stimulation and will welcome the pleasure in different positions. Use a vibrator on her clitoris while you lick her gem as well. Most women will enjoy this, just like most

Chapter Three

Alternate arousal between her clitoris and other erogenous zones, such as her breasts.

Sensually squeeze, spread, and jiggle her butt cheek while you lick.

Figure 3.11

men enjoy a woman sucking the penis and alternating between licking the penis down to the balls and back up and/or licking the balls and ass while stroking the penis. This feels really good!

More analingus techniques for her during Night Two are covered in Chapter Five, "Erotic Anal Play—Delicious Stimulation for Both of You. Use the following techniques: f. The Tongue Tingle, i. The Straddle and Flip, m. Eyes Wide Shut Figure, p. Upside Down V-Lick, and x. Bottoms Up (your tongue can lick her gem deeply, but do not slide your fingers deep inside her gem yet).

IMPORTANT: When you sensually massage her outer gem during sex, synchronize the movement of your fingers on her gem to the movement of your tongue as you kiss her passionately and while licking her neck, shoulders, and breasts. Also, synchronize the movement of your fingers to the movement of your thrusts. As you thrust forward, move your fingers over her gem smoothly from front to back.

Play and alternate, associate the creative movements of your other body parts with the sensations she is experiencing around on and her gem.

3.4 Night 3

Triple her pleasure

Now that she has enjoyed Nights One and Two, she should have a good association with gem play. **IMPORTANT:** On Night Three you are going to play with a finger and/or toy inside her gem; therefore, implement the cleaning system covered in Section 4.2. You both will know that she is clean and feel comfortable with engaging in anal play after doing so. Scan Chapter Four, Section 4.4, to see the actual images of the toys you'll use in the night to come. To start Night Three, use the foreplay techniques of Nights One and Two to arouse her with finger play and licking her gem; arouse her entire body with the activities to put her thoroughly in the mood. View them not as a means to an end but as erotic art that you are enjoying together.

Now we will dive deeper into how to stimulate **Her Pleasure Anatomy**. Lay her on her back, lick, stimulate, and play with her U-spot [**See Figure 3.12**]. The U-spot is a small patch of sensitive erectile tissue located just above and on both sides of the urethral opening, between the clitoris and the urethra, it is absent just below the urethra, in the small area between the urethra and the vagina. Less well known than the clitoris, its erotic potential was only recently investigated by American clinical research workers. They found that if this region was gently caressed with the finger, the tongue, or the tip of the penis, there was an unexpectedly powerful erotic response (Heretical.com/miscella/g-spots.html).

Start licking her vagina and clitoris. Take your middle finger, start to insert it into her vagina, and sensually circle it around her lips and play with her U-spot. Imagine all your energy flowing to your tongue and to your fingers as you continue to lick and play. Get feedback on the U-spot pressure from your tongue or finger that she likes; always ensure that every new experience feels good. In addition to her U-spot, when stimulating her clitoris, play with both sides of her clitoris, her eleven o'clock and one o'clock areas, considering her clitoris is at twelve o'clock. These are the most sensitive spots as reported by a variety of Internet articles, including Durex and Marie Claire Mag.

Now play with her G-spot. Lick your middle finger and insert it into her vagina with the soft part facing up all the way in. Bring your finger forward until you feel her G-spot toward the front of her vagina, or about an inch or so inside with a slightly padded, bumpier texture on her skin (G-spot receptiveness varies in all women. A good article was published in the LA Times, Health section titled "Mapping the Way to G-spot Utopia," (July 21, 2008) [See Figure 3.12]. Once you get there, stimulate this area using a come here motion with your fingers and in circles.

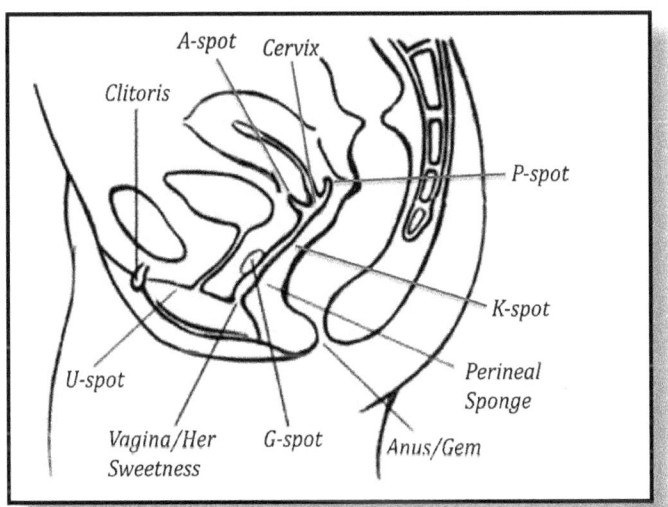

Figure 3.12

Now stimulate her A-spot (AFE-zone, the Anterior Fornix Erogenous Zone). Also referred to as the epicenter, this is a patch of sensitive tissue at the inner end of the vaginal tube between the cervix and the bladder. It is the female equivalent of the male prostate, just as the clitoris is the female equivalent of the male penis. Direct stimulation of this spot can produce orgasmic contractions (Heretical.com/miscella/g-spots.html).

Go in deep and sensually massage the top of her vagina. Turn your finger up so that the soft side of your finger is facing upward, and then bring your finger all the way up, locate her G-spot and go another inch or two backward until you notice increased feeling of pressure or sensitivity. If you sense it, good. If not, use a toy longer than your finger to reach it and stimulate it.

Next to the A-spot is the Cervix and P-spot, pictured in Figure 3.12. These spots can also give her pleasure. The Cervix is another hot spot in the vagina; it's much like a man's prostate. As you orgasm, if the cervix is rubbed properly or pounded, it can make the orgasm much more intense.

Her Ultimate Pleasure

Most men can pound, tap, or rub on the cervix because it is maybe three to four inches inside a woman. You can also use a toy such as the Slim Vibe to reach it and play with it.

Next, you can stimulate her P-spot, (Posterior Fornix Erogenous Zone); it's deeper inside at the back of the vagina on the other side of the cervix, the opposite of the A-spot. This spot is usually stimulated when a man is fully inside a woman with the correct angle. Depending on the depth of your partner's vagina and the length of your penis, you can reach it. If you are well endowed or with a toy, stimulating the P-spot can elicit intense pleasure. A position to angle your penis in the right manner to reach it is to have her lay on a couch lengthwise; since the couch is low, when you slide your penis into her vagina, you can angle yourself toward her P-spot location.

Next, you can stimulate her G-spot, clitoris, K-spot, and perineal sponge simultaneously. Lube your first finger and middle fingers thoroughly and slowly insert them into her vagina. When you go in, have your first finger massage her G-spot, place your middle finger behind your first to provide additional pressure. Massage it with a motion starting from the back and pulling toward you as if you were telling someone to come to you in a sensual manner. Put more pressure to see how much pressure she likes on her G-spot. Also, massage her G-spot in circles. Use your thumb to play with her clitoris and lick it. Now excite her <u>perineal sponge</u> and <u>K-spot</u> [See Figure 3.12].

The perineal sponge is erogenous tissue encompassing a large number of nerve endings and, therefore, can be stimulated through the bottom wall of the vagina toward the beginning of the entrance or the top wall of the rectum. Some women who experience orgasm during anal stimulation may be having their perineal sponge stimulated. These orgasms can be accompanied by ejaculation and are said to feel similar to orgasms that result from G-spot stimulation. The K-spot is opposite her G-spot and a bit farther back, behind her perineal sponge. Use the soft part of your middle finger from your other hand to massage the bottom area of her vagina, front to back and back to front. Moan on her clitoris; indulge in inspiring her moans from the arousal of a variety of hotspots simultaneously.

Once she has bigger anal toys in her gem, use the Double U technique covered in Chapter Five under the position "y" The Body Quake. This technique will excite her clitoris, G-spot, U-spot, perineal sponge, and gem while you penetrate her with your penis, possibly hitting her A-spot, Cervix, or P-spot. You'll also enjoy the vibration above and below your penis.

IMPORTANT: You are going to use the Grooves For Her Technique with lube from Night Two with a variation, I call it the **Grooves For Her Pump**. Start with several minutes of sliding your second-row knuckles up and down over her vagina and gem while licking her clitoris. Push forward gently so she feels more of the grooves from your knuckles. Then extend your middle knuckle forward and slowly push it into her gem [See Figure 3.12.1].

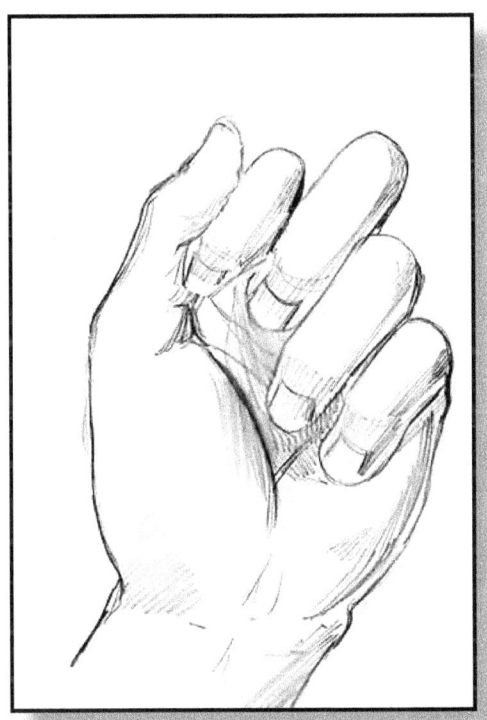

Figure 3.12.1

Since it's your knuckle, it adds stimulation without going in. Move back and forth slowly on her gem, then alternate between slow to fast pushing to excite her more. Swirl your knuckles like if you are fanning the back of your fingers into a circle on her vagina and gem as you lick and suck her clitoris.

Do the knuckles formation again: push forward slowly on her gem, hold for three seconds, and pull back; do this again and push slightly further for four seconds and pull back, go again, push further and gauge her response. Adjust for the depth that feels good to her and increase the speed of the pump of your knuckle on her gem to mimic sex. Heighten the intensity of licking and sucking her clitoris as you push your knuckle forward. This movement provides more arousal, and since it's your knuckles, there's no penetration.

Next, you are going to entice her G-spot while doing the knuckle stimulation on her gem with **The Grooves for Her Pump Variation**.

Make your hand into the shape of a gun, extend your first finger and middle finger out straight and bend your ring and little fingers to your palm [See Figure 3.12.2]. Slide your first and middle finger into her vagina and place the knuckles of your ring and little fingers on her gem. As you continue licking her clitoris, move your first finger up to apply pressure on her G-spot with your middle finger below reinforcing the pressure. Also, move your middle finger down so the bottom arouses her perineal sponge. Move your fingers in and out while your ring finger and little finger knuckles apply pressure on her gem. Move with a circular back and forth movement. Stimulating her clitoris, G-spot, and her gem will associate more pleasure to the gem arousal.

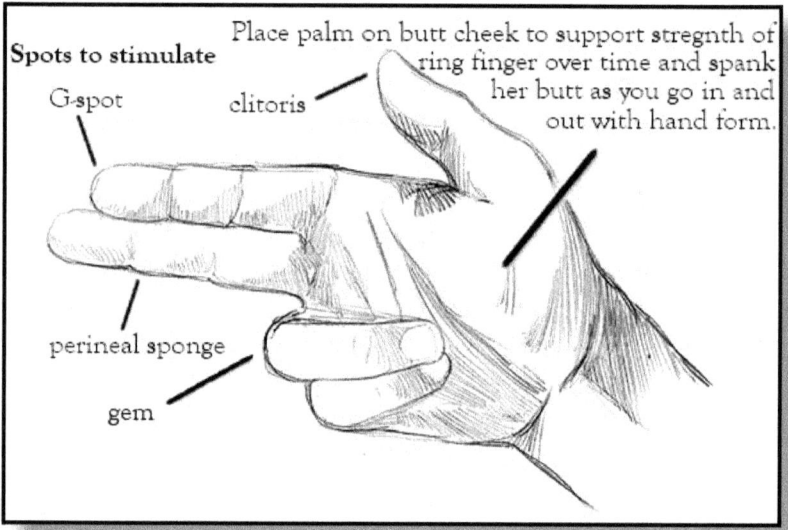

Figure 3.12.2

Alternate using the different Grooves For Her hand and knuckle movements to tease and excite her. Use your thumb to play with her clitoris, U-spot, and all around. Place your palm on her butt cheek to help reinforce the strength of the knuckles on her gem, in case they get tired from the straight forward motion. Also, as you go in and out, you can use your palm to spank her butt cheek. The spanks will produce endorphins.

Another variation of arousal with this technique is to have her lay on her stomach on the edge of the bed and you are standing on the side of the bed. Have her lift her ass up in the air a bit so she is on her knees with her knees spread. Slide one or two fingers into her vagina to massage her

Chapter Three

K-spot and perineal sponge. Lube your knuckles from your other hand and use the grooves of your knuckles to slide back and forth over her gem.

After playing in this manner, use the knuckle of your middle finger to slowly press down into her gem and push up with the finger(s) from your other hand. Your knuckle will massage her perineal sponge from the top and your finger(s) from the bottom. Massage her gem back and forth, side to side, and in circles. Mimic a pumping motion with your knuckle. All of the above will tease her gem and get her used to the pumping motion, still without penetration.

Now, you are going to lick her while inserting your little finger into her gem. Make sure your nails are well filed, or you can use a finger condom. Massage her gem with your little finger while you are simultaneously licking her and playing with two fingers inside of her vagina (use one or two fingers in her vagina, whichever she prefers) [**See Figure 3.13**].

As she starts to get more into the experience, circle your little finger on her gem, applying a little more pressure from the center of her gem to massaging outward to help her skin get accustomed to the size of your

Figure 3.13

little finger. This will serve two purposes. First, it will stimulate her. Second, it will help her gem adjust to being opened. Pour more lubricant onto her vagina and gem. With your little finger well-lubricated, use small circles and apply light pressure while slowly inserting your finger into her gem. Go in slowly and sensually to the first knuckle; pause a little until she gets comfortable. You'll be licking her clitoris and lips throughout the whole experience. Use one or two fingers from your other hand to play with her G-spot.

As you insert your little finger, wait for her to relax her sphincter muscles, about 20 seconds. The interior sphincter is a muscular ring surrounding about 2.5 cm of the anal canal near the entrance that can be relaxed to open. The exterior sphincter is a flat plane of muscular fibers, elliptical in shape, and on the outside of the internal sphincters and closer to the entrance of the anal canal. When both are relaxed, they can expand to let things through.

Next, move in and out while slowly making small circles. Continue to lick and suck her clitoris. Gauge her level of stimulation and go in deeper with your little finger to the next knuckle, and wait for her to feel relaxed again before you go further. Ask her how it feels. Getting verbal feedback along the way is important, and do so in a sexual manner. You can also switch to a small butt plug, which starts smaller than your little finger [**See Figure 3.14**].

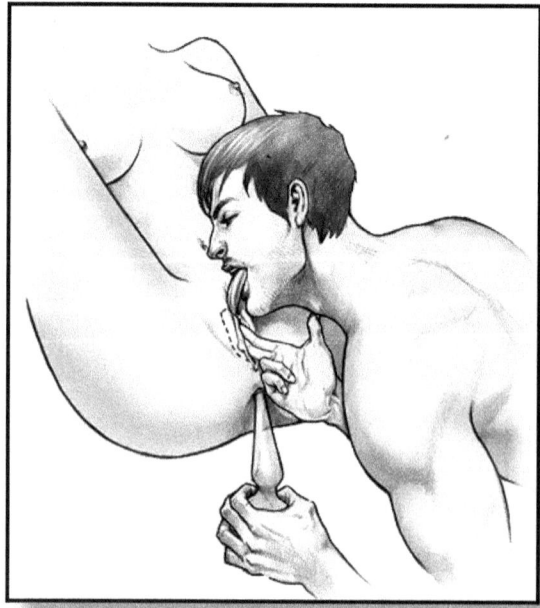

Figure 3.14

Continue arousing her with your finger. If she says it feels good, then slowly go in deeper circling your little finger. Generously pour lube on her gem before you go in further. Turn your little finger so that the soft side is up. Massage the upper wall inside her gem, where you can feel your middle finger from your other hand. As you continue to lick her clitoris, go in all the way with your little finger and play with the wall between her gem and vagina.

After some play, switch from your little finger to your middle finger. Ask her if it still feels good as you enter her gem with your middle finger. Reapply lubrication every time you switch fingers. Do not try to rush it. Suck her clitoris passionately and take the time for your middle finger as you did for your little finger. Continue to play with her G-spot with one or two fingers [**See Figure 3.15**].

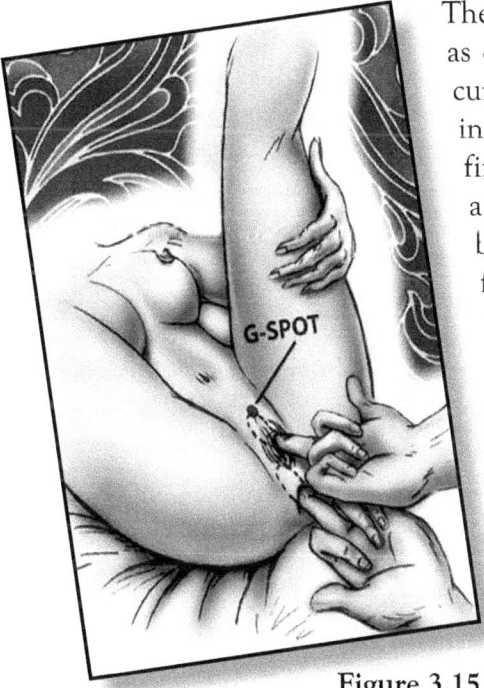

Figure 3.15

The advantage of using your fingers, as opposed to a toy, is that you can curve your fingers to provide variable internal stimulation. Also, your finger is warm. Toys do provide a smooth surface and vibration, but intimacy is higher with your fingers. I would suggest starting with your fingers if they do not bother her, then switch to a toy. If your little finger is considerably bigger than the tip of a toy that starts small and gradually gets bigger, then start with the toy.

Use small circles to insert your middle finger past your second knuckle into her gem. Go in slowly; slightly vibrate your finger. Massage all around. Now alternate back and forth penetration; as your fingers go in to stimulate her vagina, your finger is coming out from her gem, and vice versa. Send all of your energy to your lips, tongue, and fingers while you are licking and sucking her clitoris, her U-spot, and all around [**See Figure 3.16**]. Switch from alternating in and out to entering with both her vagina and gem with your fingers at the same time and going in deep. Hum, moan, suck on her clitoris with intense passion, get feedback from her that she is still feeling good in a hot manner, and continue to arouse and excite her until she has to release into an explosive orgasm [**See Figure 3.17**].

Figure 3.16

If you have the type of woman who can continue to receive stimulation during orgasm, then, by all means, continue as she orgasms. If her body becomes sensitive, then slow down or stop—but do not pull out of her gem suddenly because it might be uncomfortable for her. Let her gem pulse and squeeze your finger as she orgasms for you. Pull out very slowly after she has fully orgasmed.

Figure 3.17

Chapter Three

Another activity to do to while she sucks you is a variation of the Palm and Gem Pleasure technique from Night Two, called the **Palm and Curve Pleasure technique**. Position your hand the same way as in Palm and Gem Pleasure. Once you play on top of her gem, insert your middle finger in her gem. Move your palm up and down, side to side, and in circles on her clitoris while your finger does the same in her gem. Add more in and out action with your finger. Then add another curve of pleasure by inserting your first finger into her vagina to massage her G-spot. As she makes you feel good, get creative with this technique vibrate and pulse your palm and fingers. Lightly spank her clitoris with your palm, then massage it; use your other hand to stimulate her nipples and other erogenous zones.

More fun activities during Night Three are the techniques: **c. V-Spot Massage, h. Crisscross, l. Fingertips, and w. U-spot Love**, which are covered in Chapter Five. Then ask how she feels. If she is multi-orgasmic, then give her another by licking her and playing with her vagina or through sex. If she is not yet, then pull out slowly and let her enjoy her experience. By adding multiple methods of orgasm, she'll be multi-orgasmic in time.

IMPORTANT: Continue with sex and sensually massage her outer gem, as explained at the end of Night Two. Now, you can play inside her gem with one finger as long as it does not go deeper than the depth you have gone already. Do the **E3 and Missionary Work Techniques** from Chapter Five to insert a finger in her gem during sex.

Make sure she is not sensitive. You want the experience to always be about pleasure. Tell her the second she feels sensitive to tell you so you can stop, to prevent her from ever getting to the point of soreness or pain. As long as the finger insertion still feels good, synchronize the insertions of your finger during sex with your thrusts. Suck her tongue; as you suck it in your lips, slide your finger in, then as you sensually let her tongue go, pull the finger out in the same manner. Also, synchronize the movements above to sensual music. Let this be Night Three. Let her enjoy the thoughts and emotions of an orgasm associated with penetrative anal play. Let her relish in the pleasure that will inspire her to want more.

3.5 Night 4

Vibrate her soul

In this night, you'll add a bigger toy to help her enjoy thicker girth in her gem. Start with the activities from Nights One thru Three to arouse her but not bring her to orgasm yet. Now that she is comfortable with a finger in her gem, have her do the anal cleansing system from section 4.2 and for every following night.

Start where you have entered her gem with your middle finger, using small circles as in Night Three. Next, you are going to use a vibrating plug with a small starting girth that gradually grows in girth, either a Vibrating Plug or the Booty Call Flexer would be good. Keep her on her back, maintaining intimacy and sensual passion. Turn on the vibrator and begin to lightly stimulate her clitoris, her lips, and then around her gem. Go up and down over her gem and in a circular motion. Next, lube the entire vibrator, and while you are simultaneously licking her clitoris and fingering her vagina, slowly insert the vibrator [**See Figure 3.18**].

Figure 3.18

Chapter Three

Ask her how it feels. Does she like the vibration? Then, continue to be conscious of when you reach the point on the plug where it is bigger than your middle finger because this will be a new girth for her. Slow down and use small circles to guide the plug gradually to a bigger girth. Make sure she is enjoying the process.

IMPORTANT: Circling Techniques (CT)—the reason I suggest using small circles while entering her gem is that if you try to just press in, you'll be stretching all sides at the same time; that might feel uncomfortable. If you use small circles, the motion expands and relaxes a side at a time, giving the skin a better method to adjust [**See Figure 3.19**]. You are massaging, relaxing, and stimulating her as you insert a finger, a toy, and eventually, your penis. As you circle, you can press/pull gently in any direction for two to three seconds, then move to another direction and press/pull for two to three seconds and continue all the way around.

When making small circles slightly bigger than her gem, it should take three to four seconds to make a full sensuous circle. Do circles for at least 30 seconds to a minute, insert the toy a little more. Hold the vibrator at the new girth for about 30 seconds so that she can get used to the new girth. One hand should be holding the toy while the other is massaging the gem area around the toy while you are licking her clitoris.

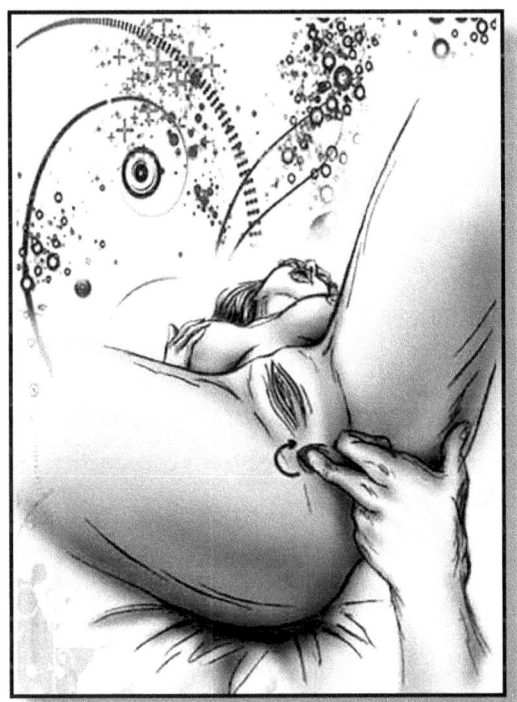

Figure 3.19

Start to play with the toy, twist it while going in and out to the new girth, and gradually increase the girth using the same technique. Do the circling and timing strategy for every inch you enter until you get a little bigger than the size of the first vibrator of the Berman Dilator Set. Now, alternate the sequence of

Her Ultimate Pleasure

entry with your fingers going in her vagina and the vibrator coming out of her gem. Stimulate her G-spot and A-spot with your fingers.

When you use a vibrating plug, it is shaped so you can go to the end and leave it in while it is vibrating to stimulate her and get her used to a slightly bigger girth. With the vibrating plug in her gem, start to play with her vagina using your penis. Tease her entire vagina area until she is begging you to enter her vagina.

Begin to enter her vagina slowly to see how she feels with the plug in her gem. This is going to feel incredible for you too because her vagina will be vibrating from the plug in her gem. Go in all the way, slowly and sensually, while playing with the plug in her gem. Once she is accustomed to both your girth and the plug, thrust more passionately. Play with the plug as you are thrusting inside her; move the plug in and out while twisting it. Continue to lube the toy to make sure it moves smoothly. Do this type of play in a variety of positions such as missionary, sideways, doggy, and her riding you.

Now instead of the plug, insert two fingers in her gem using the same circling technique. Put your first finger under your middle finger to reinforce strength, insert them sensually, and imagine sending energy to your fingers while you are licking her clitoris [**See Figure 3.20**].

Figure 3.20

To get her started on enjoying a bigger girth, switch to the smallest vibrator of the Berman Dilator Set. This vibrator is thicker than your finger, smooth, and has a similar girth throughout the length of the vibrator. Lick her and insert your fingers in her vagina, first play with the tip of the vibrator on her clitoris. Cover the tip of the vibrator with your lips surrounding her clitoris. Lick and suck her around

Chapter Three

her clitoris while tip of the vibrator is stimulating her. Use the vibrator to play with her vagina lips and inside, then vibrate the outside of her gem; adjust the vibration to what she likes. Tease her gem for a bit, then insert the tip slowly using the circling technique. You can take longer strokes with this vibrator since it is the same girth throughout.

Take the time to thoroughly pleasure her with the first size in the Berman System. Pour more lube on the vibrator, slowly take it out by doing circles as you pull back while massaging the area around her gem. Now play with the vibrating plug to a girth similar to the size of the second attachment of the Berman Set for a minute.

Put on the second attachment of the Berman Dilator System. Start by pouring more lube on the area and all up and down the toy. Lick her and kiss her all over her vaginal area. You'll now implement a new circling technique, called Circling ooohOOOHs. Start by making small circles a circumference slightly wider than her gem; have the entire circle take about three seconds and do about three of them. Now make wider circumference circles, but slower, so that it takes five seconds to do the full circle. Do three of these and three more small circles. Enter slowly using small slow circles; after an inch, hold for about 30 seconds and let her get used to the new depth girth.

During the hold time, massage the skin area around her gem by twisting your hand around the toy while you are licking and sucking her clitoris passionately. Repeat the above for the next two inches. Pull back and go back and forth to the new depth you just reached, twisting the toy while you do so, licking her as well. Pour more lube on the toy and on her gem area. Repeat everything in this paragraph to go in the length of the attachment, about four inches. Talk sexy to her, tell her how beautiful she is, how much you love pleasuring her. Then bring her to orgasm by licking and fingering her vagina. Or by inserting your penis back in her vagina while you still play with the vibrator in her gem [**See Figure 3.21**].

IMPORTANT: Now, you can play with toys or two fingers in her gem while having sex and kissing her passionately. Toys add a lot of stimulation. Do not go bigger than what she has experienced so far. Synchronize the use of the toy in and around her gem to your kissing, sucking, and thrusting during sex. Suck and circle your tongue around her clitoris and all around in the same direction as the circles you do with the toy, then alternate the direction.

Check out more fun activities during Night Four in Chapter Five: **a. The E3 Figure 5.2, d. V-Spot and Vibe Combo, k. Pearls, and u. Bend Over, Beautiful Figure 5.32**. Let that be the amount of gem play for Night Four. Talk about the experience afterward. Let her know how much it turned you on, and ask her what she liked. Also, ask her to let you know the second something is uncomfortable so you can adjust or stop for the night. Ask about the speed of inserting the plug. Was it slow enough? Does she want to try the back and forth action faster? And ask her to let you know when you are making her gem feel really good as it is happening. Hot, sexual communication about gem play during and after sex enhances the experience.

Figure 3.21

3.6 Night 5

Entering the Gem of Intimacy

Night Five is going to be very similar to Night Four, except you are going to use the next two attachments of the dilation system, other toys, and add new pleasure techniques. You'll provide more stimulation while she tries out larger girths. Soon, she'll be accustom to toys that are closer to your girth. Night

Chapter Three

Five may need to be repeated two or more times, depending on your partner's physiology and the size of your penis.

It is important that you gradually pleasure her using small increments of increasing girth so that it does not hurt her and so she keeps enjoying the process. Going too fast can lead to her stopping the process for that night or stopping it entirely. It does not matter how many times you repeat a certain night, take your time, and enjoy the process because the rewards are so worth it.

Since the dilator vibrators jump from one size to another, use a dilator plug to transition from one dilator to the next. It is about making the transition to a bigger size smooth and pleasurable. I suggest using the Berman Dilator Set because the vibrations add stimulation. Follow the process of Nights One to Four because you always want to start with arousal so that she is yearning to experience more.

While you lick her, play with the vibrating plug on her clitoris, around her lips, her U-spot, in her vagina, and down to her gem. Remember to fully lubricate her and the toy. Start with her clitoris and vagina, and then play around her gem. Only go from front to back, never back to front (in her gem to her vagina). Circle the toy around the gem and go inside. Slowly and very sensually go back and forth. Guide it to the girth that she reached on Night Four. Play around at that girth, use the circle technique, and then go in a little more until you get to a girth similar to the next attachment in the dilation set.

Put on the third attachment in the dilator set and lube it all over. Since this is a new and bigger girth all the way down the shaft that is also longer, go in slowly using **Circling oooh OOOHs and Pleasure Twists Technique** (Pleasure Twists Technique is also covered in Chapter Six). There are five steps to doing Pleasure Twists:

1. Lubricate her gem well. Put your first finger and thumb around the front of the vibrator against her ass ring, the skin area around her gem. Use the side of your first finger all the way to your thumb to massage her ring by twisting your fingers sensually around the vibrator.

2. Put your thumb in her vagina so when you twist your hand around the vibrator, your thumb goes in and out of her vagina. Massage her tang and her perineal sponge during the back and forth movement of your thumb.

3. Use the oooh OOOHs Technique to gradually expand her gem in a pleasurable way. Insert the vibrator using circling (small circles) or push down a little on the vibrator as you enter, see which feels better for her.

4. Use your other hand holding the back of the vibrator to turn the vibrator counter-clockwise and clockwise, using the opposite direction than the massage you are doing with the top hand. Also, once you have entered her gem a bit, use this hand to move the vibrator back and forth in her gem. Add lube every couple of inches.

5. Lick, suck, and kiss her clitoris, U-spot, and labia sensually and passionately so she can't help but love all the stimulation allowing the vibrator to go in her gem. Moan on her and squeeze in some hot sex talk [**See Figure 3.22**].

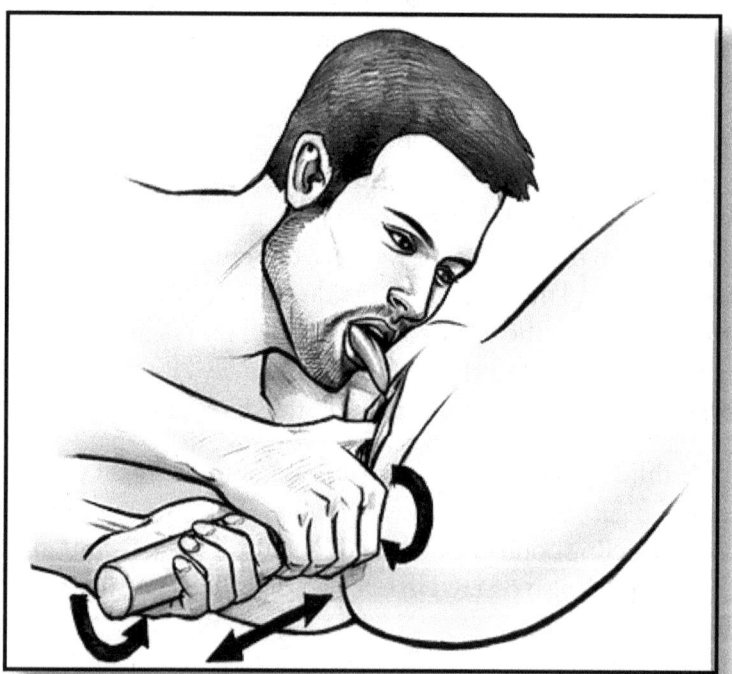

Figure 3.22

Use the above technique for every inch, stay there for 30 seconds, and perform pleasure twists and licking during that time. Do this until you reach five inches with this attachment. Perform strokes using the length that you have entered. Make her feel wonderful, tell her how beautiful every part of her body is, how sweet her vagina tastes, how luscious her gem is, how sexy she is, how much she turns you on, and play with her G-spot, perineal sponge around the toy, as well as her side vaginal walls until she orgasms [**See Figure 3.23**].

Chapter Three

Figure 3.23

If your penis is just a little bigger than this dilator, then have this be it for Night Five, in terms of increasing size. You can continue anal play with this current size during this night. On Night Six, she can take you in. So now you have taken her to the second-to-last in the set. If you are much bigger in girth—for example, if you are two inches wide—then you should do everything above again with the last dilator. Your patience will pay off by creating intimate moments where the process is so incredibly pleasurable for her throughout. She'll not only love you for it but she'll love anal play, and she'll yearn for it.

If you are much bigger than the last dilator, then you are going to need to find a vibrating dildo a little bigger than the last attachment on the Berman Set, and create a dilation system with vibrating dildos that gradually works her up to your girth and length. Repeat Night Five again for every new size past the Berman Set until you get to something that is close to your girth and length.

Show her your appreciation for every new experience. Let her know how much it turns you on. Do something sweet to thank her outside of the bedroom for being so sexy. Hold her afterward. Remember to make it an intimate experience. Get her feedback to make sure she likes how you are doing things, and if there are other things she wants you to do to her gem as well.

During Night Five, you can also use the silicone beads of a size that are similar or smaller than the girth she has experienced. You can also use a toy like the Vibrating Flexer Probe or vibrating bead toys covered in Chapter Four. Lube the

Her Ultimate Pleasure

beads, and play back and forth while you sensually massage the area around her gem and all around her vagina. Play with her G-spot, U-spot, A-spot, Cervix, and P-spot. Go in and out with the beads while licking and massaging. Insert the beads until they reach the girth she has tried, then pull them out during her orgasms. This will add a thrilling sensation to her orgasm [See Figure 3.24].

IMPORTANT: Throughout this night, take the time to kiss her passionately and arouse her other erogenous zones as you play with a toy in her gem. For

Figure 3.24

example, use her favorite attachment in the Berman Dilator Set or other gem toy; use one hand to slide it in and out of her gem while you make out with her, lick her breasts, kiss her neck, and bite her shoulders. Have her hold the toy so you can use both of your hands to stimulate other erogenous zones. Insert a vibrator in her vagina and another in her gem while you lick her clitoris. Circle the vibrators at the same time going in and out, in the same forward motion and in alternating directions [See Figure 3.25].

Now you can play with bigger toys or more fingers in her gem while having sex. Use Chapter Five positions: a. The E3, j. Good Vibes, and y. Body Quake.

Figure 3.25

Chapter Three

 3.7 Night 6

Entering the Gem of intimacy

You are now at the stage where she enjoys anal play enough at a girth close to yours where you two can have gem sex. By this time, she wants to feel the heat of your penis in her gem. And oh damn, does it feel good and look amazing! It's crucial to use the techniques in this section so as to make the entry process pleasurable and avoid any pain for her. Implement the cleaning method in Chapter Four.

Have the lubes and toys ready next to you. You should wear a condom. If you are monogamous and without disease, you can read medical articles in the Resources Section of this book to decide if later you want to switch to not wearing a condom. Prior to starting Night Six, ask her to communicate the moment she feels a slight bit of discomfort. I'll cover how to address discomfort towards the end of this night.

Do the arousal techniques of Nights One thru Five to get her really hot and ready for your penis. Do the **Grooves For Her Technique** with your knuckles massaging up and down her vagina and her gem and stimulate forward on her gem with your middle knuckle. Push your knuckle forward on her gem, first slow and sensual, then faster and deeper while sucking her clitoris.

Leave-In Technique: Get her ready for anal sex by leaving in an anal vibrator or plug that has a girth closer to the size of your penis. After arousing with Grooves For Her, lay her on her back, play with one of the bigger sizes in the Berman Dilator Set or a vibrating dildo or plug closer to your size on her clitoris and labia while you lick her. Insert it into her vagina first while you lick her clitoris, enjoy that for a bit.

Tease the outside of her gem with the toy, circle it and push forward and pull back; you are not entering yet, just teasing her gem to crave it. Then insert is slowly with the circling technique as you continue to lick her clitoris. Leave it in for four to five minutes so her gem can get used to that girth for some time. During that time, hold it in while you kiss her passionately; lick, kiss, suck, her breasts, and bite her neck, shoulders, and other erogenous zones (if she enjoys biting, start very light if she is new to biting).

Her Ultimate Pleasure

She can hold the toy so you can use both hands to excite other parts of her. Build intimacy and physical excitement. Using a plug is an option because it can stay in without holding it, but the Berman Set or dildo keeps her gem open at a consistent width throughout the toy. You can move it back and forth and maintain the same width. After trying both, my preference is one of the Berman attachments.

Have her at the edge of the bed so that you are standing in front of her at a height that you are right in front of her vagina/gem which enables more control. Put a pillow under her ass to angle her gem upward; this will enable you to stimulate more of her G-spot when you are inside. Lubricate her vagina, clitoris, and gem so she is slippery since you are going to stimulate her with your penis and hands to turn her on even more. Go everywhere with the head of your penis, in circles, and use an up and down pattern [**See Figure 3.26**].

Figure 3.26

Dip inside her warm, wet vagina and tease it. Use your hand to play with her vaginal lips and clitoris at the same time your penis is massaging her [**See Figure 3.27**].

Get creative with your fingers in a variety of patterns. Add pleasure to her multiple erogenous zones simultaneously. Remember her U-spot. Use different patterns to play with her clitoris, vagina, tang, and gem [**See Images 3.28, 3.29**]. Have your penis start the pattern and follow the pattern with your fingers. Since you are on the outside of her gem, you are not violating the "no going from gem to vagina rule."

Chapter Three

Figure 3.27

IMPORTANT: You are going to tease her gem with the **Gem Slides Technique**. Do not skip this technique; it stimulates and gets her prepared for you. Lube her vagina and her gem well. Slide the head of your penis from her vagina to below her gem. Move your penis up and down lightly at first. Then gradually start increasing pressure. Also, move your penis side to side over her clitoris and gem. Keep moving your penis up and down, adding more pressure while you stimulate her clitoris with your fingers. Stimulate her breasts and lick them while teasing her gem [**See Figure 3.30**].

Start to concentrate on her gem and apply a little more pressure. Grab the base of your penis and lightly slap the head of your penis down on her clitoris to give her a spike of oxytocin; massage her clitoris with your fingers after as you move your head down over her vagina past her gem, play up and down. Then, continue to massage up and down on her vagina and past her gem with the head of your penis, applying more pressure over her gem. Use the Gem Slides Technique for several minutes, adding pressure over her gem but NOT entering it, just teasing it so she yearns for it.

Her Ultimate Pleasure

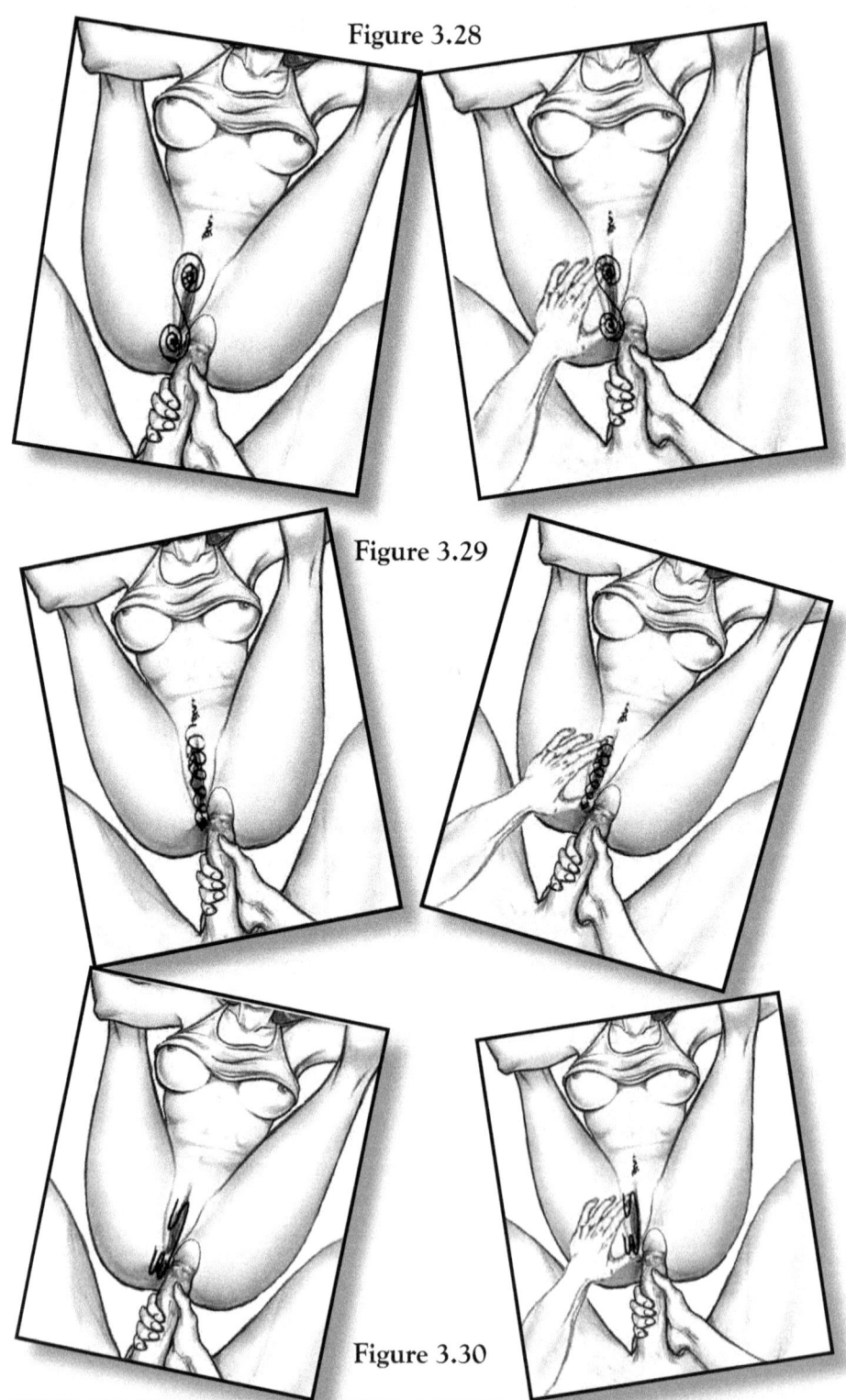

Figure 3.28

Figure 3.29

Figure 3.30

Chapter Three

To lubricate her for Night Six, you are going to implement a technique I call **Waves of Lubrication**. This technique lubricates her gem in a hot and stimulating manner. Use the Beauty Beads toy and apply lots of lube on the toy. Sensually insert the first four bulbs. Pull them out, then push

Them back in several times. Generously lube the toy again, and slide it in and out, enabling deep lubrication of the inside of her gem.

Go in as far as the length of your penis so she is thoroughly lubricated and can take you in more easily. Another option is to use the Anal Lube Shooter shown in Chapter Four, but the Beauty Beads are a sexier option for the introduction. Once she's accustomed to gem sex, the Shooter does a more thorough job. When you apply lube to yourself, make sure you cover the full length of your penis.

Figure 3.31

Now you are going to do the circling technique covered in Night Four. Grab your penis with your dominant hand and put your thumb on top of your penis to provide good guidance. You are going to make very small circles at the entrance of her gem while gradually applying pressure forward but not going in. Play with her clitoris at the same time with your other hand, or she can play with her clitoris so you can play with her nipples [See Figure 3.31]. Also, use Pleasure Twists.

Use your thumb from the hand that is holding your penis to play with her vaginal lips, and slide the thumb in and out of her vagina while the outside of your first finger massages around her gem [See Figure 3.32]. Tell her how beautiful and hot she is, how good she feels, how delicious her vagina and gem are. Circle the head of your penis on her gem.

Her Ultimate Pleasure

Then use a vibrator to play with her clitoris and vagina. The Slim Vibe works well or a Couples Dual Motor Vibrator for clitoral and G-spot stimulation or her favorite vibe. You are going to reapply lubricant to her vagina and her gem. Keep the vibrator on her clitoris, play with the head of your penis on her lips, in her vagina, around her ass, and gem.

IMPORTANT: You are going to use the **My Vibe Technique** to enter her gem. Adding vibration arouses and soothes entry. You can add vibration to your penis by wearing a vibrating penis ring like the Urnight Vibrating Penis Ring Vagina Clit Stimulator or the Adorime Penis Ring, Couples Vibrator for Penis and Clitoral Stimulation (both pictured in the toys section). These penis rings actually do make your penis vibrate. Try the Umright Vibrating ring since it has even coverage all around. It has a bigger girth circle as well. If you need an adjustable girth with a wider range, from a smaller girth to bigger, use the Adorine Penis Ring, Couple Vibrator.

To use one, lube your penis and the inside of the ring, then slide the ring to just behind the head of your penis. Grab your penis behind the toy and do some Gem Slides over her gem and vagina with the vibrating action for a minute. Slide the ring back so you can fit your hand in front of it on your penis.

The effectiveness of the My Vibe Technique comes from adding stronger vibration manually. Place your thumb behind the head of your penis, and your first and middle finger on the bottom. Replicate a vibration sensation with your penis by moving the head of your penis up and down with small movements as you enter her gem. Just like vibration stimulates

Figure 3.32

her clitoris and vagina, creating a vibration effect with your penis when inserting it into her gem will help it feel good. The vibration in her gem will ease entry because you are distributing the stretch from one side to another quickly.

During the insertion process, she is using a vibrator on her clitoris. You'll be vibrating your penis and go in slowly until your head is in, then do Pleasure Twists [**See Figure 3.32**]. Also, place your thumb in her vagina to stimulate her perineal sponge while doing My Vibe.

IMPORTANT: You'll combine multiple techniques to enter her gem, **My Vibe, oooh OOOHs, Pleasure Twists, and The Ass Jiggle Technique.** The Ass Jiggle is as follows: As you are using your dominant hand around your penis, place your other hand to cup her ass cheek and jiggle it, making a vibration sensation. Creating multiple areas of vibration arouses stimulation and enables you to enter in a comfortable and pleasurable manner. One hand will alternate between The Ass Jiggle, stimulating her nipples, mouth, neck, and other erogenous zones. Talk to her with stimulating words. Pay attention to her facial and body cues to assess your progress inward. She'll have a vibrator stimulating her clitoris at all times.

Let's start. Grab behind the head of your penis as instructed above, slowly start sliding your penis inside her gem while manually vibrating it. Once you get your penis head inside, pause and do more Pleasure Twists for about 30 seconds, do ooohOOOHs for 30 seconds, and then push the vibrating ring forward so it's flush against her skin and lips. Let her enjoy the vibration from the ring and her vibrator on her clitoris for 30 seconds.

If she says her gem still feels tight, you can try a technique I call the **Gem Relax Technique.** The two sphincter muscles in the gem have a protective response, and they just need to relax. If you tire out the muscles before you go in, the muscles will relax easier. Pull out slowly, and before you go back in, have her squeeze her gem and Kegel muscles as tightly as possible for 30 seconds. Rest for ten seconds, then squeeze for another 30 seconds. Now her sphincter muscles are tired and will relax easier. If she is feeling good, continue below. If you do the Gem Relax, start again from the paragraph above.

To continue, pull the ring back, push downward on your penis gently, and pour more lubricant on top of your penis and massage it all around

Her Ultimate Pleasure

her gem. Grab your penis and manually vibrate it as you slide it in another inch while doing the Ass Jiggle. Pause and do Pleasure Twists for 30 seconds and use your other hand to play with her nipples, massage her ass, or other erogenous zones. Kiss her passionately. Intensify connection. Push the ring forward so she feels the vibrations flush against her gem for about ten seconds. Ask her how she is feeling, does the Pleasure Twists, Ass Jiggle, and ring vibration feel good. Try different vibration modes and jiggle intensity.

Grab behind the ring, do ooohOOOHs for 30 seconds. Pull the ring back, grab your penis in front of it. Manually vibrate your penis and go in another inch while doing Ass Jiggles. For every inch you enter, pause, do Pleasure Twists, Ass Jiggles, and ooohOOOHs to let her get accustomed to the new depth.

Throughout, she has kept a vibrator on her clitoris or both clitoris and G-spot with a dual motor vibrator. You can also stimulate her clitoris with your fingers with the hand not playing around her gem. In addition to stimulating her with your thumb or pads of fingers, do Grooves For Her on her clitoris. Put all your fingers together and use your knuckles to slide side to side, up and down, and in circles on her well-lubed clitoris. Remember to dedicate one hand for clitoral and vagina play and the other for gem play.

Make sure she is feeling good before you continue and get feedback throughout. Once you get your penis to three inches of depth, slowly move your penis back and forth to one inch behind the head of your penis while doing the My Vibe and Ass Jiggle Technique for about two minutes. Place your thumb behind the depth you are going to enter. Then do Pleasure Twists for 30 seconds (**Important**, since your thumb has not touched the area of your penis that has gone in her gem, you can still slide it into her vagina. If your thumb touches an area on your penis that has gone in her gem, no longer slide your thumb inside her vagina. Or clean it THOROUGHLY with a sanitary disinfected wipe or an wet wash cloth with antibacterial soap on it before going back in her vagina.

Now grab your penis just behind the three-inch mark, vibrate it, do Ass Jiggles, and move back and forth up to the length of the three inches. Do this for a couple of minutes. Pause, do Pleasure Twists for 30 seconds, kiss her passionately, massage more lube on her gem, do ooohOOOHs. After the three-inch point, you are going to push the ring forward, flush against her gem. This time, grab behind the ring and vibrate your penis along with Ass Jiggles to go in the next inch. Yes, at three inches, I switched to having the ring forward instead. This is because the first three inches need stronger vibration directly at the point of entry. After three inches, she is now accustom to the penetration and the vibration from the ring can further soothe the circumference of her gem.

Pause, put forward pressure on the ring to vibrate her gem for ten seconds, pull the ring back. Do Pleasure Twists and Ass Jiggles. To continue, push the ring forward, grab behind the ring this time and vibrate your penis to go in further. Keep the ring forward and keep doing the above until you reach three-quarters of your length. Let that be the depth for this evening. If you go to your base, you might feel the tendency to thrust too hard. When you go to three-fourths your length, you have to pay attention to controlling your stroke. You want to ensure she feels incredible during and after so she wants more.

Continue to vibrate and Ass Jiggle, as you move back and forth. Massage more lube on her and move back and forth without the vibration to see how she likes it. Now do Ass Jiggles with the hand you had on your penis and use your hand dedicated to her vagina to stimulate her vaginal lips, clitoris, breasts, neck, and other erogenous zones. Kiss her, look into her eyes, bite her neck, do all the things she loves to create a connected and exciting experience. Enjoy the pleasure, tell her to turn up the vibration on her vibrator until she orgasms. If you are having anal sex for 30 minutes, it is best to stop at this point to play it safe so she does not get sore. Give her an orgasm, either with your fingers on her clitoris or her vibrator. You can make her orgasm quickly with a power wand or the Lelo Sona Cruise II vibrator.

It's essential to ensure you remember the techniques to make it a smooth and pleasurable experience for her. To review, follow these **Five Steps to Enter Her Gem**:

> **1. Arouse:** Lay her on her back with her butt to the edge of the bed. The bed height should be so that you are comfortably standing or kneeling (standing preferred) with your penis directly in front of her vagina, or you can use a pillow to angle her gem up slightly.
>
> Do Grooves for Her, Gem Slides, Waves of Lubrication (lubricate her vagina and clitoris as well), and Pleasure Twists to arouse her

gem. Massage her ring area with the outside of your first finger to the bottom of your thumb. Use your thumb to massage her tang and vaginal lips. As your hand turns, insert your thumb into her vagina to massage her perineal sponge.

Slide on a vibrating ring and do some Gem Slides with the vibration on high, slide the ring backward do more Pleasure Twists.

2. Enter with circling and vibration techniques: Place the tip of your penis at the front of her gem and put slight pressure on the front. Move the vibrating ring backward and grab your penis behind the head and manually vibrate it. Have her hold a vibrator on her clitoris or a dual motor clitoral and G-spot vibrator.

Vibrate your penis while you do the ooohOOOHs Technique, three small circles slightly wider than her gem ring that take three seconds around, do another three circles a little wider circumference that take five-seconds, and three small again, three seconds around. Continue to vibrate your penis as you very slowly slide your penis in just past your head. Get her feedback and adjust for her comfort.

3. Pause and stimulate: Pause for 30 seconds to let her adjust to you. During pause time, do Pleasure Twists, using the outside of your first finger to massage around her gem and lips, sliding your thumb on her tang into her vagina to stimulate her perineal sponge. Pull out your thumb to play with her U-spot. Kiss her sensually and passionately, and use your free hand to arouse her clitoris, breasts, and other erogenous zones.

Push the vibrating ring forward flush against her gem again. All the while, she is stimulating her clitoris with a vibrator. Massage more lube on her. Pull the vibrating ring back and grab your penis half an inch behind your head and do ooohOOOHs.

4. Add Ass Jiggles and reinforce sensual connection: Manually vibrate your penis again, do Ass Jiggles, and go in another inch. Pause, repeat Step Three. Continue to go in using Step 2 with Ass Jiggles and Step 3 at after every inch until you get to three inches deep. At three inches, pause, stimulate and start to slowly move back and forth, manually vibrating your penis and doing Ass Jiggles for the length two inches for about two minutes. Then to three inches for two minutes.

Place your thumb behind the insertion depth. Pause and do Pleasure Twists for another 30 seconds. As you do them, make sure your thumb does not touch the insertion area on your penis since you started back and forth action. If it did, do not insert it in her vagina. Clean it thoroughly first with a disinfected wipe.

Reinforce connection by kissing her passionately, her lips, neck, shoulders, and look into her eyes. Use the hand dedicated to her vagina to massage her clitoris with lube, and your other hand to massage lube around her gem and on your penis.

5. After three inches, switch the vibe ring to the front position, continue forward repeating steps 3 and 4, and enhance arousal: To go further, switch to having the ring forward, grab behind the ring to vibrate yourself and enter another inch, repeat steps three and four for every inch you enter until you get to about three-fourths of your length. You want to maintain a pleasure high, and going into your base might lead to hard thrusting. Leave that for the next night. Continue to kiss and enhance connection. Raise the intensity of passion with hot sex talk, and arouse multiple erogenous zones, her breasts, etc.

Every several minutes of going in and out for minutes, massage lube around her gem. Make the entire circumference feel good. Keep adding lube periodically throughout the whole process. It feels soothing to her gem and adds stimulation.

During all the above activities, use your other hand to simultaneously play with her vagina, U-spot, G-spot, breasts, nipples, lips, neck, legs, and feet. Use your mouth to exhilarate her body wherever you can reach. Do not do the plain back and forth movement you see in videos. Move with sensuous rhythm to the music playing in the background with your licks, bites, fingers, and body thrusting. Yes, it requires a lot of multitasking, but it's the most fun multitasking in life.

Playing drums, playing guitar and singing, or engaging in other activities that help condition your body to do a variety of different things simultaneously increases your multitasking skills. Tap your head, circle your hand on your stomach, do the moon walk, shimmy your shoulders, and sing the Star Spangled Banner! Joking, but do engage in activities that will help be a multitasking master. You want to be able to do many activities simultaneously while in sync with her sensual movements.

Her Ultimate Pleasure

As you go inside, imagine your souls wrap around each other, breathe together, and flow together in that experience. Send all your love or care to her with every kiss. Imagine energy going to your fingers and your penis. The more physical AND emotional pleasure you create, the more she'll enjoy it.

Figure 3.33

To enhance emotion, keep the vibrator in place as you lean forward to kiss her breasts, bite her neck, look into her eyes, and kiss her passionately. Support yourself well so you do not accidentally thrust deep inside of her while you are leaning forward. She can hold her clitoral vibrator or lay it between your bodies so it stays on her clit. Let her know how good she feels wrapped around you, and how much she turns you on. In this intimate and passionate position, you can use the back of your fingers instead of the vibrator to stimulate her clitoris, U-spot, and G-spot [See **Figure 3.33**].

Ask her what feels good. Does she want slower or faster? Though you are not going to pump hard on Night Six—that is for Night Seven. Night Six is to get her to enjoy her first gem sex experience with your penis inside her gem. Patience is pleasure. Take long sensual strokes. Guide the progression with continuous feedback and make the dialogue HOT!

Stop using the clitoral vibrator and massage lubricant on her vagina and clitoris with the hand with no gem play. Massage more lubricant around her gem with your other hand. Lean forward, lying close to her. Reach around and massage her gem with your fingers as you go in and out of her so that you pleasure her gem from the outside as well as the inside.

The finger technique is as follows:

Figure 3.34

1. First finger massages the bottom side of her gem.

2. Middle finger massages her upper gem and her tang.

3. Ring and little fingers massage her clitoris and the inside and outside of her vagina [See Figure 3.34].

You can also insert one or two fingers into her vagina to stimulate her (make sure it is not the same fingers that were playing with her gem or keep hot washcloth with soap to clean your fingers prior to this move). On another night, when you can go all the way in her gem, pour lube all over your pelvic area, so when you are lying on her, your pelvic bone will slip and slide over her clitoris as you thrust.

Ask her what is more likely to make her orgasm, the vibrator on her clit or your fingers there or a combination. Do what she prefers until she has an explosive orgasm while you are inside her gem and receiving all the other pleasure at the same time. Stop thrusting, let her enjoy the feeling, pause for her to get accustomed to the sensation post her orgasm. As I stated earlier, if you are getting close to 30 minutes and she has not orgasmed yet, pull out the big guns and use a power wand or the Lelo Sona Cruise II, both can provide an orgasmic mic drop!

If she does not have an orgasm after 30 minutes of gem sex, then let that be it for the penetration action this time. Leave her wanting more. If she has orgasmed from anal play during the previous nights, then she'll most likely orgasm if you focus on her pleasure.

If she does orgasm from gem penetration and you feel like you are going to orgasm at the same time as her, take the following into consideration. If you have a thick penis that gets bigger toward the base and expands a lot from pulsating when you orgasm, then pull out slowly to just before the head of your penis before you orgasm. You do not want your large circumference close to your base inside her gem, it can expand too much during your orgasm and can hurt her on her first anal penetration experience. You do not want her to experience any pain, so be thoughtful of her gem and gradually position your penis to where it does not expand a lot.

IMPORTANT: After she orgasms, STOP thrusting, let her enjoy, and thoroughly relax. Yes, even if you have not orgasmed. You want her feeling good and not get sore from her first time from too much activity. Many times, a woman gets more sensitive after orgasm. You want nothing but great sensations associated with the experience.

When you are ready to come out, DO NOT PULL OUT FAST. Pour more lube on her gem. Push the vibrating ring forward, so it is flush on her gem. Let the vibration soothe her for a minute or two. Put a vibrator on her clitoris and manually vibrate your penis as you come out. If you pull off the vibrating ring, massage around her gem doing the Pleasure Twists, then manually vibrate your penis and pull out very slowly. She might be sensitive, so be smooth on the exit. Remember to talk about the experience and get her feedback. If you did not orgasm from gem penetration, still make her orgasm orally or with vaginal penetration.

If she let's you know that she feels discomfort, immediately stop. Pause for a minute until she feels comfortable, try the My Vibe Technique without moving in and out. If she still feels the discomfort, stop, that is it for the evening. Pull out very slowly using the exit strategy mentioned above. Her pleasure and comfort are always top priority, even if you'll orgasm soon, stop, orgasm with vaginal sex, or in another manner. If the tables were turned, you would want the same. Try again on another night and do more teasing. Use toys closer to your girth and length to prepare her gem prior to you going in. Excite her gem even more with the Grooves For Her and the Gem Slides Techniques until she is begging you to go in. Arousal is where you need to shine.

Chapter Three

You two are now able to continue expanding the amount of activity and positions you can do with anal sex. Night Seven will cover how to go deeper and faster while using more positions. Plus, I'll cover more ways to stimulate her during anal sex..

3.8 Night 7
Hear those magical words you've been waiting for, "Give me more, more!"

Night Seven! Now you'll experience a variety of positions. You'll also start penetrating and thrusting more as you do with vaginal sex. As with every night prior, set up ahead of time to create the mood, include music and lighting. Enjoy implementing the stimulation techniques from Nights One thru Six. Use different toys to stimulate her. Use the silicone beads or Vibrating Anal Beads Butt Plug to get her ready for anal sex.

If the woman your with can orgasm multiple times, you can give her an orgasm before you begin anal sex to relax her. If she has one or two intense orgasms, then build up the excitement but hold off on making her orgasm until you're engaged in gem sex. At the edge of the bed, start in the missionary position to build intimacy. Put a pillow under her butt, bend your knees a bit so you can angle the head of your penis upward, and you'll be able to deliver even stronger stimulation to her G-spot. Follow the techniques in Night Six to enter her gem. Stroke in and out while pulling your penis upward to excite her G-spot [**See Figure 3.35**].

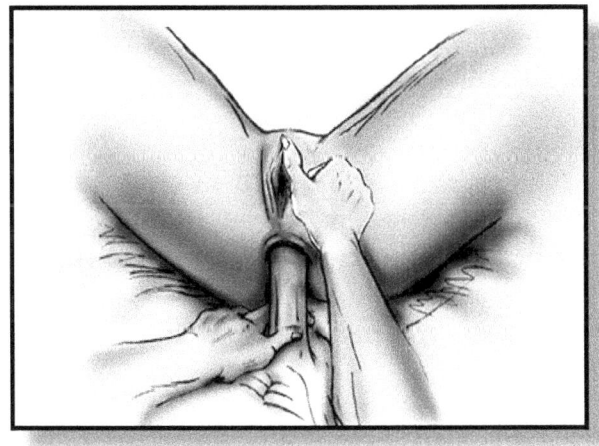

Push your penis downward and see if it is pleasurable. Continue to grab your penis to pull up, push down, pull side to side, and do circles as you stroke in and out. Get feedback from her to see what feels good, what angle and pressure she prefers.

Figure 3.35

Do the My Vibe Technique but increase the range of vibration more side to side and up and down. Indulge in the things she enjoys. Remember to maintain clitoral stimulation on her at all times with a toy or your fingers. Insert your thumb in her vagina to massage her G-spot and the soft side of your first and middle fingers to massage her U-spot and clitoris [See Figure 3.36].

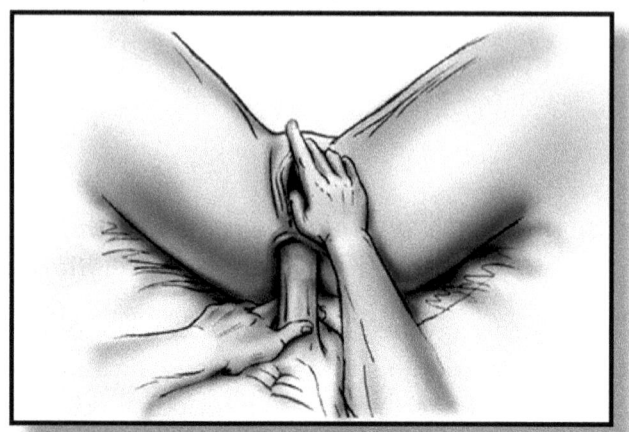

Figure 3.36

Apply a good amount of lube to help keep the stimulation slippery and wet. Have her hold a toy on her clitoris. Massage her vagina with one hand while the other hand massages the area around her gem as you slide your penis in and out. Do the Grooves For Her technique on her clitoris. See if she can take it deeper with stronger thrusts. Bring her torso up and passionately bite her neck, create intensity of excitement in other erogenous areas. The oxytocin release will enable her to experience the intense stimulation anally as well. Give her a hot experience full of sexual variety. Play with her nipples and passionately kiss her as you thrust deeper into her beautiful gem! If she likes her nipples squeezed or having your hand erotically around her neck, then do so while engaging in passionate dirty talk to heighten excitement.

Now you are going to change positions. Grab one of her ankles and lift her leg so her foot is pointing to the ceiling [See Figure 3.37].

Enjoy this for a bit, and then put her legs to the side so she is on her side. This position enables you to enter at different angles; try a variety of angles, and especially try angles that will stimulate her G-spot. Use your hands to stimulate her vagina, her perineal sponge, G-spot, labia, and clitoris. Spank her if she likes it. Spanking releases endorphins to heighten arousal. Balance the spank by sensuously massaging her ass. Become a master of the biophysical factors of arousal.

Use the Ass Jiggle Technique, squeeze her ass cheek sensually and jiggle it. The jiggle/vibration motion increases stimulation. Do ass and vagina

Chapter Three

Figure 3.37

massage as you are going in and out of her gem. Spread her ass cheeks to give you more access to this area [**See Figure 3.38**]. Suck her toes and do Grooves For Her with swirls, vibration, and pulsation movements. Have her join and spread them for you so you can use your hands on other erogenous zones.

In the beginning, it's important that you continue stimulating her clitoris and anal ring while engaging in anal sex. When she is accustomed to anal sex, you can use both hands to give her stimulation in other ways too. Put both hands on her nipples, or one hand touching her lips while the other is massaging her G-spot. Remember to only use the non-anal play hand on her clitoris or around her mouth.

You can do all the positions you would do during vaginal intercourse. Apply lubricant frequently.

Figure 3.38

Her Ultimate Pleasure

Whatever goes in her ass first cannot go in her vagina, not fingers, toys, or your penis. This rule is covered in Chapter Four. For every new position, go in slowly to ensure that the angle is okay for her. When entering her in a new position, use the vibrator on her clitoris.

There are certain positions where you can use your pelvic bone to provide the clitoral stimulation. For example, if she rides your penis with her gem while facing you, put lots of lube on your pelvic bone area and lots of lube on her clitoris and pelvic area. Position a small pillow under your butt to lift your pelvic bone higher. While she rides you, angle her upper body so that her clitoris is being massaged against your pelvic bone as she moves back and forth. Join the movement as long as the rhythm is enjoyable to her. Use both your hands to spread and shake her ass cheeks back and forth and in circles.

Put your hands on her waist to move her around. Then, pull her in closer. Reach around and massage the outside of her gem sensually, and use your fingers as follows:

Right-Hand

1. Use your first and middle fingers to massage the backside of her gem ring.

2. Use your little and ring fingers to massage and play with her gem ring and tang.

Left-Hand

1. Use your first and middle fingers to massage the other side of her gem.

2. Use your ring and little fingers to massage her vagina and her clitoris

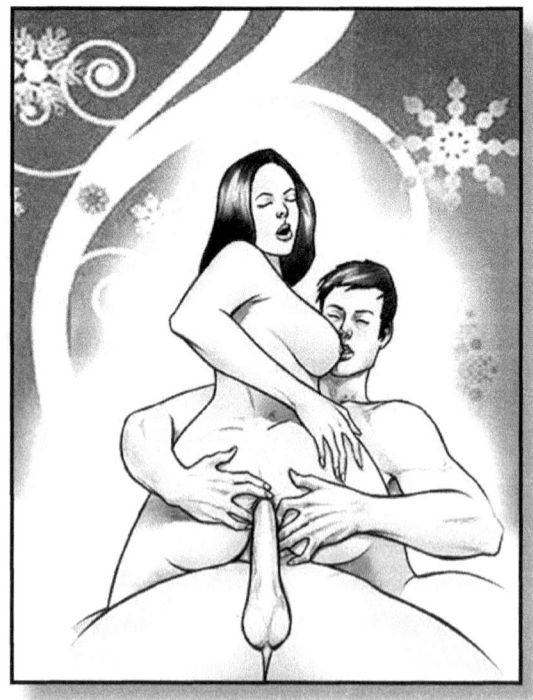

Figure 3.39

Chapter Three

(designate these fingers for vagina play only, and do not use the gem play fingers for playing with her vagina) [See Figure 3.39].

To enhance the riding experience, use a technique I call **Ride The Grooves**. Lube the back of your fingers/knuckles and lay them flat over your pelvic bone, so the knuckles are facing up. Turn your knuckles so they are in alignment the direction of her clitoris down to her labia. The grooves from your knuckle will provide more stimulation, adjust the curvature of your knuckles for her pleasure. Slightly wave your knuckles as she rides you back and forth.

A variation of the **Good Vibes** technique in Chapter Five is to put a vibrating penis ring on and have her sit on you with her gem ring flush against the toy. Her weight on the toy will intensify the vibrations. Also, when doing gem missionary position, slide your penis all the way so that the vibrating ring is pressed against her gem, and make out with her.

Now you can start engaging in a variety of positions. Use toys, plugs, and vibrators in her gem while you are in her vagina. Also, use toys on her clitoris, U-spot, and in her vagina to stimulate her in inner pleasure spots while you are in her gem (but remember, don't go from back to front, wash them thoroughly).

Once she's accustomed to anal sex and she's willing to prep for gem sex, especially if you are well endowed, try the Leave-In Technique with a plug; compare the feeling between a plug and a Berman attachment. She already knows anal sex feels good, and she'll welcome experimentation. As stated above, I prefer Berman attachments; the first time you enter her gem because you don't want to experiment in the beginning. The Berman has proven to provide pleasure consistently because of the vibration and smooth, consistent girth. Remember to continue to stimulate her everywhere else while arousing her gem with the leave-in toy.

Now that she is enjoying gem sex, use **Tantric Techniques** to increase the intensity of her orgasms. Arouse her to the point of almost having an orgasm with any type of play but then decrease the stimulation, so she does not orgasm yet. Do this several times to build the intensity of her arousal, then on the fourth time, arouse her while having gem sex, and she'll have an explosive orgasm! You can also build her up several times with anal play and have her explode on the fourth. Gauge her gem sensitivity, make sure she does not get sore from lots of gem play. With time, she'll be able to do more and more.

As she becomes accustomed to anal sex on a regular basis, continue to do the stimulation techniques and the My Vibe technique – manual vibration of your penis to enter her gem. The vibration soothes entry and adds stimulation. Review the Hand Quake technique in Chapter Five.

In summary, it's better to take your time throughout the process because if you go too fast and you hurt her, you'll most likely bring a stop to the progress. It will be hard for her to trust you again. Do not mess up and create a situation where you need to ask for forgiveness. Put yourself in her shoes: How would you like it if she got revenge on your butt by doing what you did to her? I'm sure your butt is clenching up right now. Yep, mine is as well. So don't rush; take all the time that she needs.

Focus on enjoying the journey, building trust, and making her pleasure and comfort top priority. Love to make her feel amazing! You'll both savor one of the most erotic and intimate acts in sex. She'll relish in the intense full-body orgasms! In Chapter Four, I cover preparing for anal sex, toys, and lubes. In Chapter Five, I describe a variety of positions, use of different toys, and finger pleasuring strategies that you can use to enhance stimulation and add variety to your new-found erotic delight.

Chapter Summary

Chapter Three ~ 7 Nigths to Ecstasy

Enjoy the Process of Pleasuring Her, and Give Her Thrilling Orgasms Every Little Step of the Way

3.1 The Process In Detail

How to perform every touch, lick, and caress

a. View every night as art you'll create together and stop at the designated points to entice her to want more.

b. If she is interested in anal sex, have the woman your with read this book; it is designed to arouse her to want to try the system for the pleasures she'll enjoy.

3.2 Night 1 *Beginning a new world of pleasure*

a. Pleasure her by stimulating only the outer gem with your finger while licking her clitoris and her vagina. Implement the SEPOR Method.

b. Lick, suck, and kiss all of her erogenous zones before you play around her outer gem, kissing her passionately all over: neck, shoulders, arms, breasts, stomach, pelvic bone, sides, thighs, calves, feet, and toes. After that, start licking her sweetness.

c. Tell her in a hot, sexual manner during the foreplay that you want to massage around and over her gem and that you have no intention of inserting your fingers in her gem; you just want to caress her entire body to excite every inch of her. This is important, so she knows what to expect, and she won't be scared of you trying to insert your fingers when you caress over her gem.

d. As you lick her clitoris, use your hands to massage her thighs, lips, around her vagina, the area between her vagina and gem (her tang), then around her gem, but not inside. That is as far as you are going to go for anal play on Night One. Bring her to orgasm while doing this.

3.3 Night 2 Feel the warmth of my passion

a. Start with Night One techniques and implement the SEPOR Method. As you sensually and passionately lick her vagina, move down to her tang. Lick and kiss there, tease her, and come back up to her clitoris.

b. With hot, sexual talk, let her know you want to caress her gem area with your tongue, and you have no intention of inserting your fingers, just stimulating her gem area to see how she likes that. Tell her you want to send all your passion to your tongue and lips, and that you want her to experience that around her gem. It's important that she knows what to expect so she is not scared.

c. While you do that, massage the outer gem with your fingers, then go back down closer to her gem and come back up continuously to stimulate her outer gem. Keep doing this until you're sensually licking around her gem and playing with her clitoris at the same time. Continue to move up and down from her clitoris to around the gem. Then sensually stay licking around her gem and let the warmth of your tongue slightly go in the center of her gem while you play with her clitoris. Use the Grooves For Her Technique to arouse her vagina and gem while you lick her clitoris passionately.

d. Thoroughly enjoy doing this for her. Then combine that with what you know will bring her to orgasm. Reaffirm—talk about what she liked, could have modified, or anything that she might not have enjoyed as much.

3.4 Night 3 *Triple her pleasure*

a. Start with the techniques of Nights One and Two to excite her. Express the erotic art of your souls (read the second paragraph of Night Three).

b. You are going to lick her clitoris as you slide your middle finger in her vagina to massage her G-spot. Lubricate her gem well and play around her gem area. Use the Grooves For Her Technique to arouse her. Then slide your little finger to the first knuckle, pause, allowing her to get more relaxed and comfortable. After she has adjusted, then continue.

c. Using the Circling Technique, go to the second knuckle. Let her relax and feel comfortable before you go farther. All of this is happening while you are simultaneously licking her clitoris and massaging her G-spot.

d. Slide two fingers into her vagina so you can cover a larger area of her G-spot or massage her G-spot with one finger and her perineal sponge with the other finger. Continue to lick her clitoris.

e. Review the illustrations of Night Three. After you use your little finger to play with her, do the same process for your middle finger. Make sure you reapply lubricant.

f. You can use the V-Spot Massage and the Crisscross Techniques, as covered in Chapter Five.

g. SEPOR—get lost in this moment, and you'll reach the O and then perform the R.

h. Play with her gem during sex.

3.5 Night 4 *Vibrate her soul*

a. Start with the techniques of Nights One and Three to arouse her. During this night you are going to insert a vibrating toy with a slightly bigger girth than your finger into her gem.

b. Before playing with her gem, use the vibrator to play on her clitoris, play around her vagina, inside her vagina, stimulate her G-spot, and perineal sponge.

c. Use the Circling Technique to enter her gem.

d. Slow down when you get to a girth that is bigger than your middle finger because that is where she left off. Go slower at this point, using Circling, and pausing every half-inch to let her get used to the new girth.

e. Use the ooohOOOHs Technique to enter her gem with the base vibrator from the Berman Dilator Set. Let her relax and feel comfortable before you go farther inside of her. All this should happen while you are simultaneously licking her clitoris and massaging her G-spot.

f. Review Night Four's illustrations. After you play with her using the base attachment, put on the second attachment from the dilator set. Reapply lubricant and use the Circling ooohOOOHs Technique.

g. Use fingers and toys in her gem during sex. Perform the V-Spot Combo Massage Technique, as covered in Chapter Five.

h. SEPOR—get lost in this moment and you'll reach the O and then perform the R.

3.6 Night 5 *Expand her ecstasy*

a. Start with the techniques of Nights One thru Four to arouse her. During this night you are going to insert a vibrating toy with bigger girth that is closer to the girth of your penis.

b. Use the Berman Dilator Toy with the first additional attachment, as you did on Night Four.

c. Before playing with her gem, use the vibrator to play on her clitoris and play around her vagina. Inside her vagina, stimulate her G-spot and perineal sponge. Use the Circling, oooh OOOHs, and Pleasure Twists Techniques to enter her gem with the Berman Dilator Vibrating Toy. Have her enjoy this while you lick her clitoris and massage her G-spot.

d. Put on the third attachment to the Berman Dilator and do as item (c) above. But this time, slow down because this is a new, bigger girth than she has had before. If you are bigger, use the last attachment of the Berman Set and repeat item (c).

e. Additional variations include using a vagina vibrator on her clitoris as you enter her gem with the Berman Dilator. You can use a G-spot vibrator as well. If you are well endowed, you should repeat Night Five on another night with a toy that is closer to your girth.

f. Other fun activities during Night Five are the Good Vibes position and the U-spot Love Technique covered in Chapter Five.

3.7 Night 6 Entering the gem of intimacy

a. Start with the techniques of Nights One thru Five to arouse her. On this night you are going to insert your penis into her beautiful gem using a variety of techniques. Use the Grooves For Her Technique.

b. Lubricate her vagina and gem well. Stimulate all of her with your penis using the illustrations provided throughout Night Six.

c. Use the Gem Slides Technique to tease her so she yearns for you to enter.

d. Use the Waves of Lubrication Technique to thoroughly lubricate her gem so she can take you inside smoothly.

e. Use My Vibes Technique in combination with ooohOOOHs, Pleasure Twists, and Ass Jiggles Techniques to enter your head. If she feels tight, use the Gem Relax Technique, and then start pleasuring her again.

f. Use all of the techniques above to enter an inch and pause at every inch to let her get adjusted. Wait for about 30 seconds or so. Tell her that you are going to pause, and when she is comfortable, to let you know by saying "YESSS," then continue. Reapply lubricant at every inch, to make sure she is fully lubricated. Review the Five Steps to Enter Her Gem.

g. Look into her eyes, kiss her, tell her how beautiful she is, how sexy she is, and how good she feels. Enjoy every moment.

h. She is trusting you with her gem, and you need to treasure it. Keep the focus on her pleasure. Don't try to pump her hard and fast right now; that will come in time. She'll be having multiple orgasms from gem sex soon, if you progress with patience.

i. Once you are halfway or more inside, put lubricant on her and your pelvic area. Lean down to have your chest close or next to her breasts. Position a vibrator on her clitoris so it continues stimulating her. As you go inside farther, kiss her with all your passion. Create a very intimate experience the first time you enter her gem.

j. Use slow and sensual movements. Night Seven is when you'll do more positions and engage in deeper thrusting. You want her to enjoy this time and not be sore afterwards. Enjoy the intimacy for a while. Implement the SEPOR method at the end and give her an orgasm. Give her a break at twenty minutes to a half-hour. Night Seven is just around the corner, and you two will have even more fun then.

3.8 Night 7 *Hear those magical words you've been waiting for, "Give me more, more!"*

a. Start with the techniques of Nights one to six to arouse her.

b. You are now in her gem, and she is on her back on the edge of the bed. Angle your penis in different positions to invigorate her G-spot and her other erogenous areas.

c. Get feedback as to which directional pressure she likes. Continue to simultaneously stimulate her clitoris.

Chapter Three

d. Lift one of her legs up, and angle her to the side. Then, put both of her legs together to one side. Use your hands to excite her vagina, perineal sponge, G-spot, labia, and clitoris.

e. Heighten her endorphins by spanking her. Use The Ass Jiggle Technique. Play with her nipples, caress her body, and hold her neck as you kiss her. Talk dirty and/or passionately, or whatever turns you two on.

f. Ask her what speed and depth feel best for her. Do that only; do not thrust much deeper inside of her more than what you have gotten her used to. You don't want to mess up now after all the time you put in. You'll be able to go deeper and faster soon enough if you are able to do it carefully and listen to her now.

g. Remember not to place toys, fingers, your penis, or anything in her vagina after they have been in her gem.

h. You can do any position that you do in vaginal sex when having anal sex. When she is riding you, use a pillow under your butt to accentuate your pelvic bone and/or lube the back of your fingers/knuckles and place them over your pelvic bone to thrill her clitoris.

i. Focus on enjoying the journey, building trust, and making her pleasure and comfort top priority.

Chapter Four

Preparing for Pleasure

Making Anal Play Good, Clean, Fun

4.1 Hygiene

Making the pleasure zones delicious and safe for ultimate delight

One of the reasons some couples do not engage in anal play is because of the hygiene factor. They're concerned is the area might not be fully clean. I'll cover how good hygiene for anal play can be attained in a fun and pleasurable way. To engage in anal play for Nights Two thru Four that involves gem licking, both partners have to feel comfortable and know that the area is clean, safe, and ready for play.

You can make the act of cleaning the gem a pleasurable, intimate, and erotic experience. Here's my method of cleansing for Nights Two thru Night Three. The next time you two are going to have fun, I would suggest taking a shower or bath together first. Make a sexy experience out of it. Light candles and play sensual music. You can start with a bath to relax, and then turn on the shower. I'll cover the shower example. Have fun soaping each other up and down. Lather her sensually, kissing her and caressing her body with liquid soap. Lather your chest thoroughly, and then lather up her breasts with your chest. Use antibacterial shower gel to lather the lower half of her stomach all the way down and around to the top of her gem.

Chapter Four

The cleansing process offers another chance to delight her with pleasure. Warm, soapy water feels really good when it is being caressed on your erogenous zones and all over you. Work up a lather, then start with her front. Turn her so your chest is lathering her back, reach around to caress her breasts, stomach, thighs, and everywhere in between. Kiss her neck, and if she likes biting, bite the area between her neck and shoulder, gently then deeply. You know what turns her on, so do what she enjoys. If you are not into sensual biting, I recommend you try it. It transfers a lot of intensely erotic energy, and like spanking, it releases oxytocin.

Sensually move your hand and fingers to play with her vagina. After some of this titillation, stand to her side, lather both of your hands, and start caressing and washing her backside and her front simultaneously. Have your fingers meet in the middle, and massage back and forth to wash her. Put Balneol Lotion (see back of chapter) on your little finger to wash the middle of her gem. Use the Finger Roll Technique to put soap on her gem and arouse her. Push in lightly with your little finger. First, just put a little pressure on the outside of her gem so you get your little finger barely inside to about mid fingernail, so she is clean for when you lick her gem sensually later. Make sure your fingers are well-manicured, filed,

Figure 4.1

Her Ulitmate Pleasure

with no sharp hangnails. Remember, you are not trying to penetrate her deeply yet, just wash her.

Once you get to Night Four, you'll cleanse her gem passed your second knuckle. First, your little finger, then your middle finger. Make small circles with your little finger in her gem. If she feels good with that, try very slowly to go to your second knuckle. If you have a thick little finger, try her little finger first. After she is used to anal play, you'll be able to put in your whole little finger, then increase to your middle finger [**See Figure 4.1**].

Once she is really into anal play and you are able to go deep into her gem, then she'll implement a more thorough cleansing system covered in the next section. If you do not have a chance to take a shower together, then ask her in a sexy manner if she'll clean herself during her shower because you want to indulge in licking her all over for a long time. If a shower is not possible, then have her wash up with soap and use baby wipes when she is washing up for you. As her comfort with anal play increases, you can ask her to put her finger inside because you'll be licking her gem intimately.

Cleanliness is definitely a very important part of anal sexuality. If she is confident that she is clean, and you know that she is clean, then you can completely enjoy gem licking and feel good about the hygiene factor. There are many good shower soaps that leave you smelling good. One I recommend is **Clean On Me**. If the woman your with shaves herself well, she can fully feel the warmth and wetness of your tongue and it lends to easier cleanliness since it eliminates the chance of bacteria staying on hair. It is like if she were to lick your scrotum that has lots of hair, you would not feel as much of her tongue on you as you would if you shaved your scrotum. Also, it would be more pleasant for her to lick you without the possibility of hair ending up in her mouth.

If you want her to lick your gem, then you should shave and clean yourself for her to lick you. You want to make it pleasurable for her to lick you. Check yourself to make sure you smell good under your scrotum and your ass. If you both want to keep your hair, no problem, just ensure your hair is clean. Get a lotion or oil that smells good and tastes good, or has no taste, but make sure you smell good and taste clean. Products I recommend are **Hempz Original Herbal Moisturizer, Hempz Sweet Pineapple & Honey Melon Lotion, Proclaim Professional Care Natural 7 Oil**, and

Chapter Four

Making Love Massage Oil, Strawberries and Champagne. You want her to yearn for you to lick her, and for her to lick you. Then you two can enjoy a Gem 69.

4.2 Clean Up for Anal Play

To indulge in gem sex, cleaning the gem inside is the best strategy. A system to clean the gem is to use an **anal douche bulb** filled with warm water to flush out the gem. This helps later to greatly reduce the chance of anything coming out when you enter the gem with toys or your penis. There are anal douche bulbs you can buy on the Internet, or you can go to your local drug store and buy an anal douche bottle for three dollars. Make sure you get the bottle with the largest capacity. Uncap the douche bottle, do not use the contents, empty it, and flush out the liquid with water until the bottle is clean. The day before an anal cleaning, she should eat fiber-rich foods.

When performing an anal douche for the first time, she might not find it sexy since she does not know what it will feel like. To make her first cleaning experience good for her, make it a sexy experience. Set up the ambiance similar to the Night Two to Three experience above, put candles and music in the bathroom. Put slightly warm water in the anal douche bulb or bottle and lube the nozzle. Have her take off her clothes and clean with a baby wipe. Standing behind her, kiss her neck, her shoulders, bite her neck, and make out with her. Lube her gem with the Finger Roll Technique covered in Night Two. Starting with your little finger behind her gem and waving your fingers up sensually. Arouse her in this manner for a bit.

Once she is lubed, slide the tip of the bottle in her gem slowly until it's fully inside. Slowly squeeze the bottle so you don't send a rush of water into her. As you squeeze the bottle suck, kiss, and sensually bite from her neck to her shoulder. Before the bottle is empty, slowly pull the bottle while squeezing water out until you get to the front of her gem. The force of the water coming out of the spout will cleanse the beginning of the canal as you pull it to the entrance.

Her Ulitmate Pleasure

Step out of the bathroom so she can sit on the toilet and let the water come out. If it is not fully clear, have her wipe with a baby wipe and repeat the steps above until the water is clear. Wait for ten minutes, and do it one more time. Then have her take a shower and soap thoroughly; have her put soap on her little finger and go in to the second knuckle, twist her little finger some and back and forth until the entrance is thoroughly clean for you to lick. Cleanse with water, and she is good to go for delicious gem licking, play, and sex.

Once you and your partner are into having anal sex regularly, there are stronger and quicker options for cleansing, like the traditional **red enema bag** and shower attachments that will do a stronger cleaning. With shower attachments, be sure to watch the water temperature. You don't want it hot; lukewarm is fine. With the red enema bag, read the directions carefully. Do not raise the bag up fast and high, or you'll have a tidal wave of water going in the bum fast and furious. You can also use a shower attachment, which enables efficient washing.

A thorough cleansing system that a woman can use to make sure that she is completely ready for hot anal sex is the following:

1. Use glycerin suppositories (you can get these at any drug store chain). Don't leave the house until you get the urge to go to the bathroom.
2. After you use the suppository and go to the bathroom, use an anal douche as instructed above, and repeat until water comes out clear.
3. Then use unscented baby wipes to deeply wipe and cleanse the genitals and anal area.
4. Take a shower, use a soap that does not irritate you or a genital cleanser like **Balneol, Organyc Intimate Wash, or Summer's Eve** and rinse the area and your gem well using your finger, done. Use a nice smelling soap like **Clean On Me** as a final step.
5. If some time passes before you actually start the fun, do a baby wipe swipe right before to make sure you are clean.

4.3 Other Hygiene and Health Considerations

As I stated in Chapter Two, my purpose with this book is not to replicate what other resources have done well on topics of anal sex. There are resources on the Internet that offer good information of explaining anal health issues, and they can provide more in-depth content on this subject.

Go to the **Resources** section of this book and find subsection **Anal Sex Health Research**. There, I provide a variety of books and links to more in-depth research on anal sex health, anal anatomy, and anal sex Q&A articles published by medical and resource websites.

As pleasurable as anal sexuality can be, you have to put in the time to learn about the health aspects of engaging in the act. If you are going to thoroughly lick her and enjoy anal play, you have to make cleanliness a must. If you don't, it can possibly lead to health issues. Millions of couples use good cleanliness, enjoy anal sexuality, and are fine. Check out the additional resources to understand anal health.

Also, when you are engaged in full-on anal sex and discover that a little fecal matter has made a surprise appearance, know this: it's no big deal. Just clean it off with a baby wipe. It is the human body; ensure that you make her feel comfortable and that it is no problem at all. Reassure her that it is alright and that she does not need to feel embarrassed.

Another aspect in hygiene is fingernails. Make sure you cut your nails and file them so they are very smooth. The gem is very sensitive to little edges and hangnails, so file well; if you feel the edges, she will too. You can also use finger cots. They are little, finger-size condoms that help prevent your nails from scratching her gem internally.

One very important point clearly made in all the books on anal play, and which must be reiterated, is that you should not go from playing in her gem back to her vagina area with anything (this includes fingers, toys, and your penis). You should not finger her ass and then use the same finger to play with her clitoris or the outside of her vagina or the top of the area of her urinary opening. Do not use the same hand/fingers that are playing around her gem to play with her clitoris or vagina. You can use finger condoms or latex gloves while you are playing with her gem area, and take them off to play with her clitoris. If she fingers her own ass or yours, she should not play with her vagina.

You can go from vagina to gem, but you cannot go from gem back to vagina. You can clean your fingers with soap and water, then rinse thoroughly. Or clean your hands with antibacterial wipes. Use baby wipes for wiping genital areas, but make sure the wipes do not have irritants. Make sure she does not ever wipe with a washcloth or baby wipe from back to front. Do not reuse a washcloth in the same evening. Have her urinate after sex. The above is to prevent her from getting a Urinary Tract Infection (UTI). HealthLine Magazine provides **9 ways to reduce the risk of a UTI**. Commit to being diligent about good health practices.

If she goes through a thorough cleansing routine, you can play with less risk of mishap. **I recommend designating one hand for gem play and the other hand for clitoris and vagina play.** Millions of people enjoy anal sex without any health issues—you can too! The content in this book does not guarantee safety; the techniques are my best practices for providing a safer experience.

I would also recommend wearing a condom the first several times you try anal sex with someone who is new to anal until she is really well versed in a thorough cleansing process. Men can also catch a UTI, unless she is thoroughly clean. Once she has done anal enough times, and she is doing a full cleanse, then it is up to you to do your research on the health risks before you make a decision on going in without a condom.

Chapter Four

4.4 Toys for Explosive Anal Orgasms
Making the process completely pleasurable

You can give her incredibly explosive anal orgasms and make the process painless with the right use of toys. Toys are an important part of making the process of anal play orgasmic for her so she loves it and yearns for it! You'll love that she loves it, so it is worth spending the money for the right toys, lubes, and whatever else it takes to make it a fantastic experience for both of you.

To arouse a woman to enjoy the process of gem play, you'll need a toy with the right shape. The perfect toy is one that starts very small in the beginning and gradually gets bigger in girth. It is made with smooth material that is safe for anal play and has the option to vibrate. After extensive research, I found some toy options that provide lots of pleasure and help her enjoy the eroticism of a toy stimulating her gem.

There are two types of stimulation that you need to do on her so that the process feels good at all times. The first is using a toy to stimulate her clitoris and vagina. The second is using a stimulating toy to enter her gem. The first can be a normal vibrator, but it is preferable to have one with strong power and variable speed settings so that she can adjust it to feel exceptional for her. The second toy for her gem, as I described above, also has features to prevent it from fully going into her gem. There are a large variety of anal toys on the market; I am going to focus on the ones that are intended for a beginner and for incorporating erotic anal play into your sex life.

Below are toys and lubricants that I recommend for pleasurably introducing a woman to anal play. Throughout this book I'll describe when and how to use them.

If you do not have a butt plug or a mini vibrator, then the product I recommend you start with is a **Vibrating Plug** [Image 4.2]. It starts small and gets bigger, it is soft, and it vibrates. "A silicone butt plug with a vibrating bullet will have you smiling from cheek to cheek. Slip the waterproof, wireless, vibrating bullet into the soft silicone plug to relax muscles and

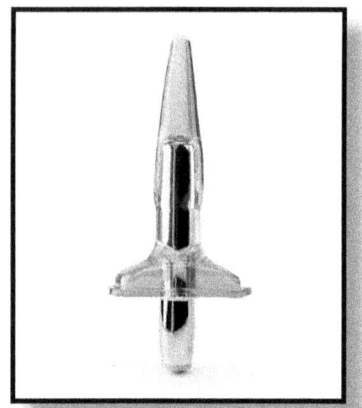

Image 4.2

provide extra stimulation or slide it out to set your other pleasure points abuzz. It is silicone, so it is safe for anal play." The perfect toy would be longer and gradually build to a bigger girth, but this product is good for beginners because it is small and stays relatively slim throughout the length. It takes one AAA battery.

The Petite Sensations Teazer 7 Speed Anal Vibrator [Image 4.3] is another vibrating toy that is thin and therefore great for introducing gem play. The Twist will allow you to go where you haven't gone before. The easy-to-clean material and friendly size make it a great option for those new to anal play as it's non-intimidating. Dimensions: Insertable Length: 3.875 inch (plug) and Width: .4 inch(tip). Since this toy is longer, you can move it back and forth with strokes in and out. It takes one AAA battery.

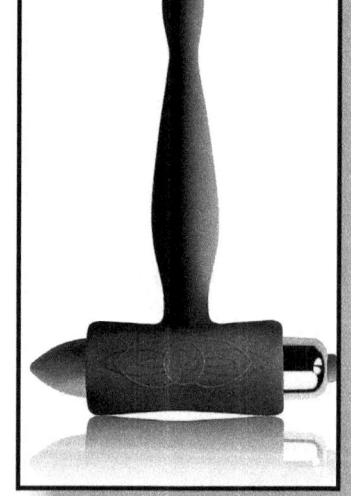

Image 4.3

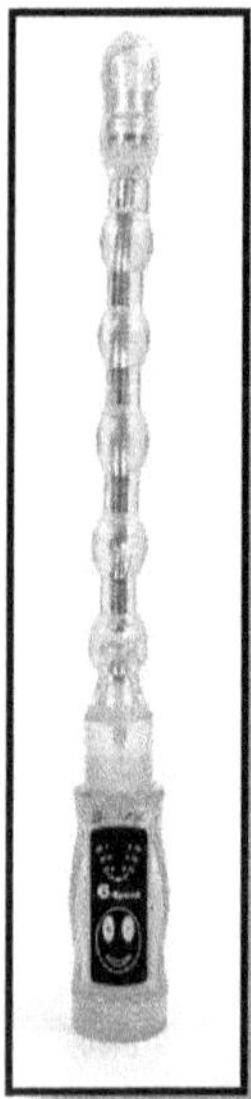

The Eden Vibrating Bendable Anal Beads [Image 4.4] has stronger vibrations at the insertable tip so there is more stimulation at the point of initial insertion. It has a 6 1/2" insertable length with moderate intensity a diameter: 5/8" takes three AAA batts. **The Booty Flexer Vibrator Probe** [Image 4.5].has more intense vibrations, a diameter of 1" and an insertable length of 3 1/2". Beaded probe flexes and is multi-speed. It takes two AAA batts.

Image 4.4

Chapter Four

If to expand the plug circumference, you can get the **Vibrating Anal Plug Training** [Image 4.6], Internet description: "With a silky texture, comfortable and sleek appearance and exciting swirl. Ability to warm quickly to your body. Designed for you to experience the true delight and enjoyment of adult toys! Plug 1 has a width of 1.1 inches, plug 2, 1.3 inches, and plug 3, 1.5 inches. USB rechargeable.

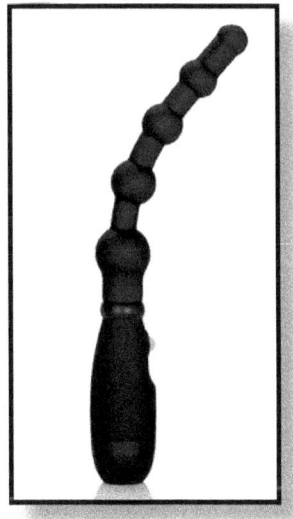

Image 4.5

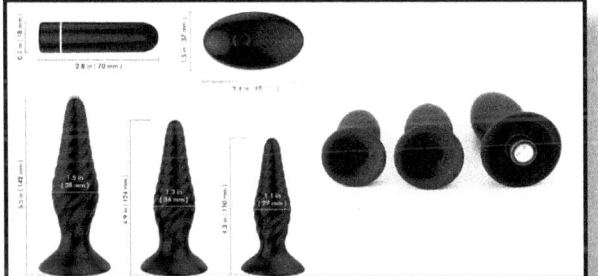

Image 4.6

Get the beginner dilation set called the **Berman Dilator Set** [Image 4.7]. It is a set of vibrators starting from a small girth to large girth. If you have a very thick and long penis, you should get this set. **Buying this set is a must** because it allows you to take longer strokes in and out with a consistent girth. Also, some other dilation sets do not have the flared handle to prevent the toy from going all the way in.

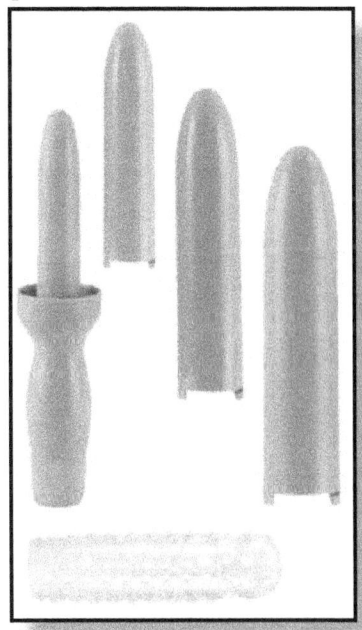

Image 4.7

Internet description: "This vibe is four vibes in one (think: Russian Nesting Dolls!). Designed to help with dilation, this vibe is great for those who may have medical reasons for wanting a versatile toy with graduating sizes. What's different about this dilator is its powerful multi-speed vibrations, adding more pleasure to the mix. With interchangeable, interlocking sizes, this hard plastic vibe is comfortable and smooth to insert. The set includes four sizes (3 ½" x 7/8", 4 ¼" x 1", 5 ½" x 1 ¼", 6 ¼" x 1 ½") and one silicone-blend sleeve that fits the smaller sizes. Takes two AA batts.

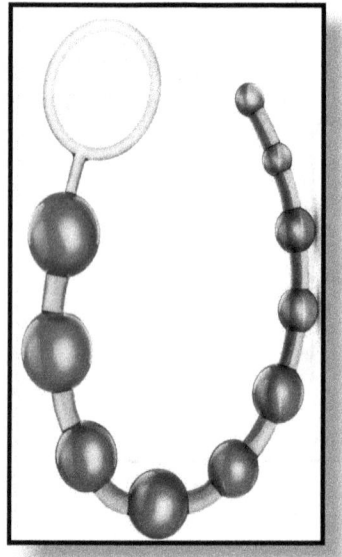

Image 4.8

Beaded toys provide a unique type of pleasure, and you can get one that does not vibrate or one that does. The ones that do not vibrate are usually longer and provide more stimulation when pulling them out during orgasms such as **Silicone Beads** [Image 4.8] (in multiple colors). Internet description: "Smooth and soft; these beads are graduated, so you can start slowly and have fun working your way up." These are used in the Waves Of Lubrication technique. Also, during sex you can insert them in her gem and pull them out as she orgasms. A vibrating option for anal beads that start very small and increase gradually is **Doc Johnson Sliders Multi-Speed Rippled Anal Beads- Style Vibrator** -8.5 inches long [Image 4.9].

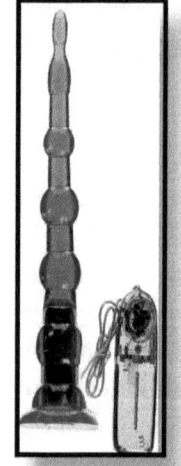

Image 4.9

Doc SlidersThe next type of beaded toy is a vibrating one for additional stimulation. Vibration is amazing for making many things feel good. The curved beads vibrate along the length of the toy. This toy is called **Triple Explosion Vibrating Beads** [Image 4.10]. With this toy, you can get her used to thicker levels of girth with strong vibration with the stimulation of gradually bigger beads. Internet description: "3 powerful motors deliver 10 vibration modes in 3 intensity levels each.

Chapter Four

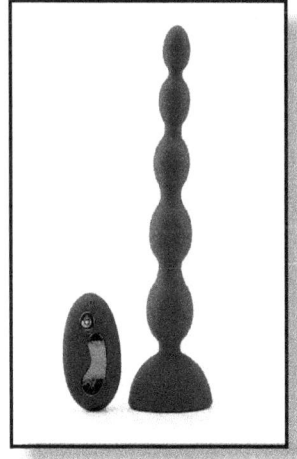

Image 4.10

The remote control allows for easy adjustments; Made from the body-safe silicone; USB rechargeable and waterproof. Use this toy while licking her clitoris while playing with this toy in her gem and another vibrator in her vagina. Or during sex while she lays on her side or is in a bent-over position.

Another variation of toy for later in the process is called the **Vibrating Anal Beads Butt Plug** [Image 4.11]. This toy has a handle to make it easier to push back and forth. In a bent over position, you can insert it in her gem, and while having sex, you can put your thumb through the hole and manage back on forth action of the toy easier than others. It has ten vibration modes. USB rechargeable. You can use this toy in her gem while having gem sex or in her vagina while having gem sex.

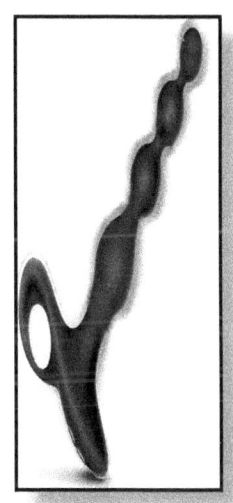

Image 4.11

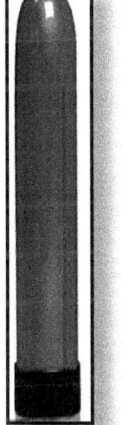

Image 4.12

You should purchase a good vibrator for her vagina, clitoris, and everywhere play. Two popular options are the **Slim Vibe** [Image 4.12]. It is both versatile and powerful. Description: "Waterproof, with a powerful motor and a stylish metallic finish. Slim, smooth, comfortable, and multi-speed! Great beginner toy, typically 6" long, 1" in diameter." The Slim Vibe is easy to manage and takes batteries, so if it discharged, just replace the batteries as opposed to waiting for a toy to charge. I advise having at least one battery-operated toy so you don't have to wait for a toy to charge in case you want it immediately. Takes two AA batts. Another good vibrator is the **G Spot Vibrator for Vagina Stimulation by LuxeLuv** (#1 vibe on Amazon- right side) [Image 4.13].

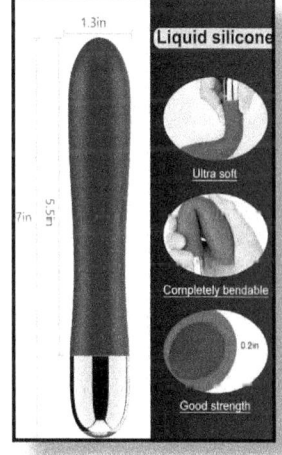

Image 4.13

Her Ulitmate Pleasure

<u>Couples Vibrator with Dual Motors 10 Powerful Vibration Modes for G Spot Clitoral Stimulation</u>, more options are the <u>Lelo Tiani 2</u> and <u>WeVibe</u> **[Image 4.14]**. It's made of a material that glides easily on your skin without pinching. It has ten different settings ranging from steady vibration to pulsation. During anal sex she can experience hands free thrilling stimulation to her clitoris and G-spot! You can use your hands to stimulate her other erogenous zones. This type of toy works best when she is lying on her back; gravity is keeping it in place. USB rechargeable. The WeVibe and LeLo Tiani 2 are two more versions of this toy.

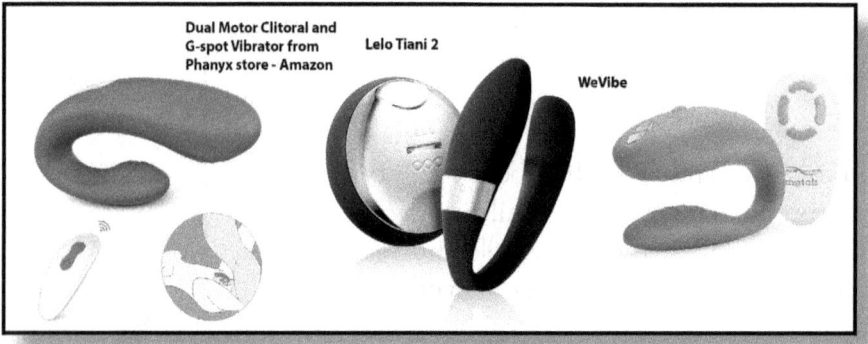

Image 4.14

Use this toy during anal sex. If you insert with the small end into her vagina to stimulate her G-spot, you might have to hold it in place with one hand. It might stay in on its own. Another method for using the toy is to insert the big side into her vagina to stimulate her G-spot, and the small side vibrates her clitoris. This method tends to keep the toy from moving around.

Also, see how she likes the big motor in her gem while the small motor stimulates her perineal sponge while you have vaginal sex. You might have to keep one hand around your penis close to her gem to keep the toy in. Additionally, you can insert the big motor in her vagina while the small one goes in her vagina while you have sex. To stimulate her gem, perineal sponge, G-spot, and her clitoris during vaginal sex, use two of these toys at the same time. The big motor goes in her gem, small in her vagina, and the second big motor on her clitoris and the small end on her G-spot then slide into her vagina. I call this the Double U technique covered in Chapter 5 under letter Y. Body Quake. USB rechargeables.

To stimulate her clitoris, U-spot, G-spot, and perineal sponge while you have gem sex, use this toy. It has two bigger bulbs. You can use the <u>Remote</u>

Chapter Four

Control Wearable G-spot Clit Vibrator, 9-Speed Clitoral Dildo Vibrator [Image 4.15]. When you insert the bigger bulb into her V, it will stimulate both her G-spot, perineal sponge, and K-spot. The outside bulb has to dots

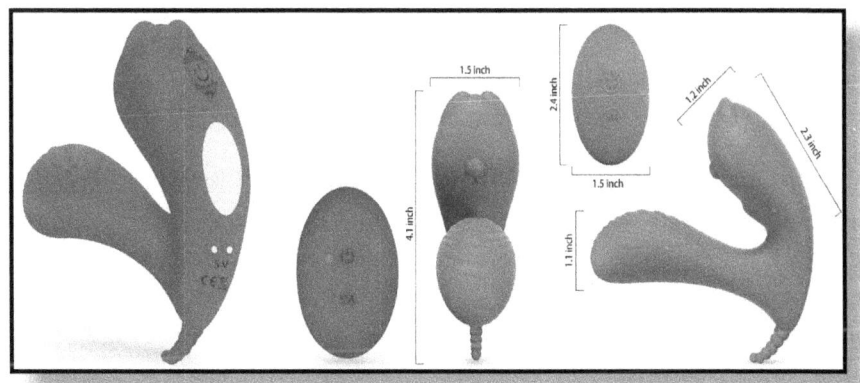

Image 4.15

of stimulation one on her clitoris and another on her U-spot.

The little tail goes in her gem. It is small of enough for you to enter as well. See how both of you like the feeling of the little tail. If you don't like it, you can just put it to the side or cut it off if you don't want it at all. Cutting it won't disrupt the function of the other parts. Waterproof Medical Material. Quiet & Silent Vibrator—Less than 40 decibels when it vibrates to give you quiet stimulation. Give her the remote so she can play with the vibration modes. USB Rechargeable.

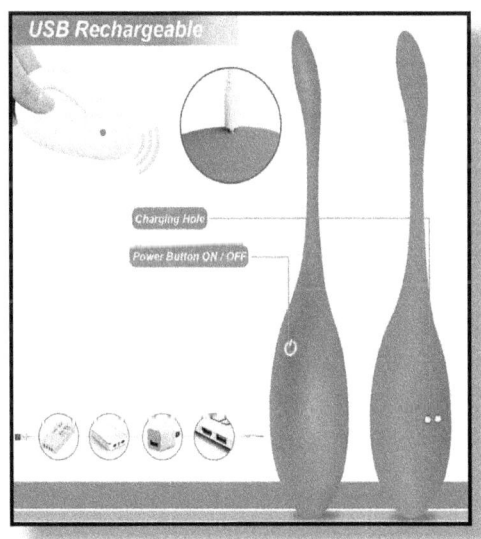

Image 4.16

Another method to stimulate her G-spot and perineal sponge during gem sex is to use vibrating kegel ben wa balls. It is shaped in a manner that hits all the spots mentioned, and she can use a vibrator on her clitoris. The SheLins Kegel Exerciser [Image 4.16] on Amazon, is one that's not expensive and has a decent number of reviews. The sex benefits of exercising Kegel

Her Ulitmate Pleasure

muscles for women are that she can improve blood circulation to her vagina and pelvic floor. This can help increase sexual arousal, making it easier for her to reach orgasm, as well as increasing vaginal lubrication (wetness).

Wireless remote control to exercise your pelvic floor muscles in different modes. Use this toy in combination with a vibrator on her clitoris. There are a variety of variations of this toy; some have two bulbs and some sync with your phone. USB rechargeable.

This toy makes your penis a vibrator, the **Urnight Vibrating Penis Ring, Sex Toys for Men, and Couples clit Stimulator** [Image 4.17]. Vibrations soothe and stimulate; therefore, she'll feel better when you are entering her gem. It is part of the My Vibe technique covered in Night 6, though manually vibrating your penis takes priority because you create stronger vibrations through your strength. The diameter across the inner circle is 1.65 inches and it stretches.

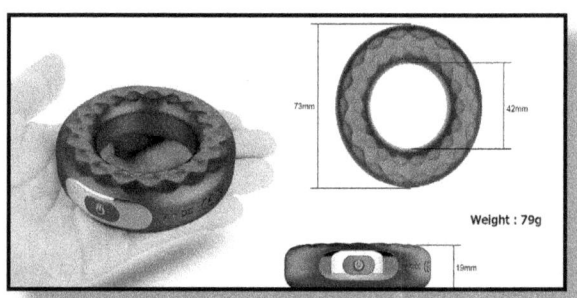

Image 4.17

Since the shape is the same all the way around, you don't have to worry about its position. It can twist, and you are good. The circumference will also soothe her when it is flush against her gem. Wear it during vaginal sex, and it will stimulate her clitoris. This is a good toy for when she is riding and grinding on you since she'll be consistently feeling the vibrations. It has ten modes and is USB rechargeable.

If the diameter of the ring above is too big or not big enough. Use the **Adorime Cock/Penis Ring Vibrator with 9 Powerful Vibrations** [Image 4.18]. It has a smaller diameter, and since it can open, a man with a bigger girth than the Urnight above can open it to fit. The inside of the ring has raised lines to help it stay in place, which can also enhance stimulation. There are 9 Vibration Modes. This one has a wireless remote control. Give the remote control to your woman! USB rechargeable.

During vaginal sex, the ends are shaped to arouse her clitoris. During gem sex, face them towards you so you have an even surface even if it twists.

Chapter Four

Place the heavy side of the toy on the top of your penis; it will stay on easier. The vibrations are stronger on the Urnight toy above, and since there is no opening, it will not fall off regardless of how much action happens. It is my preferred choice if the girth works for you.

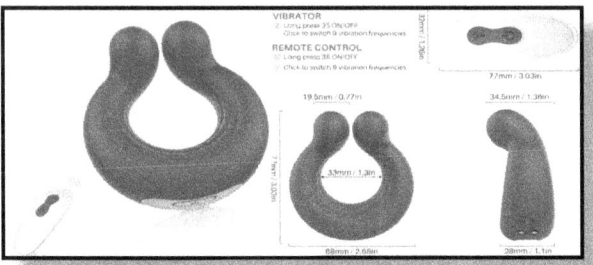

Image 4.19

Now for a relatively new technology in the toy market. **The Lelo Sona Cruise 2 [Image 4.20]**, this tech stimulates the entire clitoris—even the parts you don't see—with gentle sonic waves instead of conventional vibrations. It is stated to stimulate 75% more of the clitoris through technology that replicates the feeling of being next to a big speaker at a club and the music goes through your body.

Many online reviews from women state that it brings them to orgasm extremely quickly. Yes, I can attest to witnessing its power to do that. I would recommend using this toy once you are having gem sex, and you want her to experience an extremely strong orgasm, probably quickly!

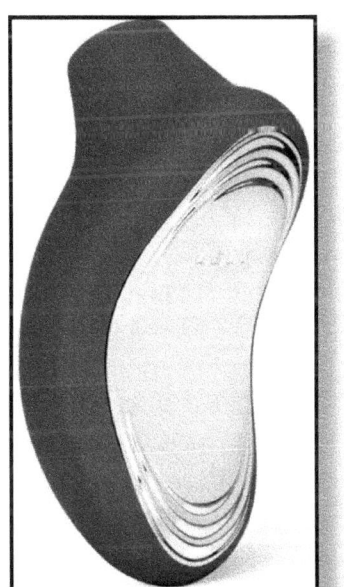

Image 4.20

Last but not least, the toy used in the Body Quake position in Chapter 5, the **Cordless Personal Wand Electric Massager** [Image 4.21], or a similar massager. These types of massagers are very powerful. They will leave her with a long-lasting, full-body smile. Internet description:

"It has a soft, spherical head and gives a soothing massage. Speeds from "That feels so good" to "OMG, I'm cumming!" Use this toy in combination with others and alternate toys.

Her Ulitmate Pleasure

Due to its intensity, if you only use this toy consistently, the body will get used to the intensity and other toys might lose their potency in comparison. USB rechargeable. There are others on the market that plug into the wall. The ultimate in electrical power. You can compare to see which you prefer. I do like the cord versions because of their power; get an extension cord to get you freedom to move around. Though, I recommend starting with a USB version and assess whether you need more power. The move anywhere feature of a USB powered device is valuable.

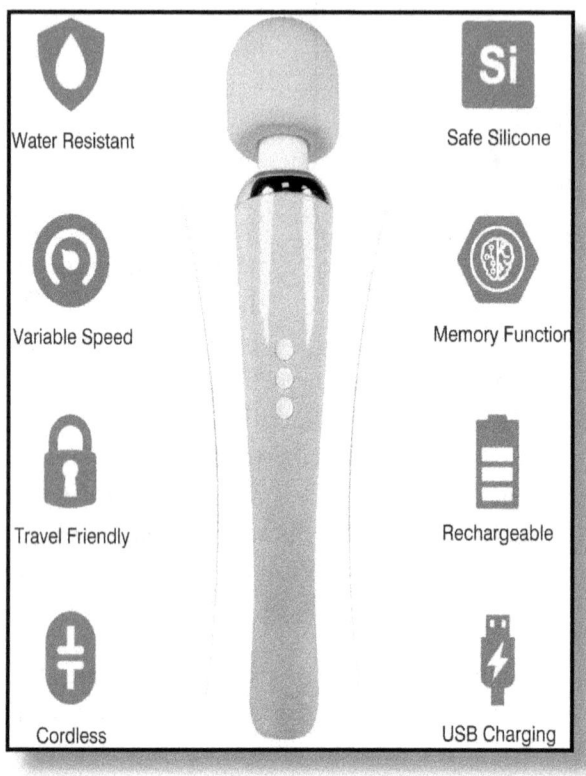

Image 4.21

Toys are an important part of the process for introducing a woman to anal sex. First, a toy should start very small so that it is comfortable for the woman. Second, stimulating her clitoris while engaging in anal play and entering her Gem will allow her to enjoy the process more and cum throughout the process. Third, **always wash your toys well with toy cleaner/cleanser before and after you use them. At the minimum, you should get the small vibrating butt plug, the Berman dilator set, a vibrating penis ring, and the slim vibe (if she already has a vibrator then use hers instead of the slim vibe, make sure it is strong)**. The plug and the dilator set well enable you to introduce penetration with a very small size in diameter to gradually increasing to a size to is close to the average man.

Chapter Four

4.5 Lubricants
Enabling wetness to take her to new worlds of pleasure

Lubricants are the magic potions that enable you to bring her to new heights of ecstasy. There are many types of lubricants, and finding the right one will take some experimentation because taste or feel is a matter of preference. I tested a variety of lubricants. I'll explain the different kinds, provide my preferences, and give you a few options.

I want several benefits from my lubricant. First, the consistency has to be right: not too oily, not too thick, because it will feel like you are putting goo on her. It should not be too thin or watery because that type usually does not last long enough, especially for sex-sessions that last for hours. I like a lubricant to feel like an extension of her wetness. It might be slightly thicker when you put it onto your fingers, but once you massage it around, it should feel close to her wetness, or only slightly thicker to maintain lubrication for lots of motion.

Second, for when you are licking and massaging her gem or performing the Grooves For Her technique, it should taste good. It does not have to be sweet but good enough for you to really indulge in kissing her, sucking her, and licking her for a long time.

Third, the dispenser needs to be convenient and functionally reliable. Get a dispenser that is small enough for you to work with one hand. Get one with a system that lets you dispense easily, not a big Costco bottle but a dispenser that looks cool, not too big, and not so small that you could easily misplace it during sex. Have two bottles next to you for efficient reapplication throughout the process, and just in case one falls where you can't see it.

I started with Astroglide for sex because I liked the consistency. Then I had a girlfriend who was irritated by the glycerin in it. So I tried silicone-based lubricants because they are supposed to last longer with smaller amounts. After trying Eros, which supposedly has a big following because it is silicon, I found I did not like the consistency of the lubricant. It was too thick, and it felt oily.

Those two products represent the two types of lubricants available: oil/silicone-based lubricants and water-based lubricants. The water-based lubricants come with and without glycerin, flavored, and in cream form. I'll focus on the water-based lubricants because I like the consistency better for anal sex. Water-based lubricants do not damage condoms, and they clean off the body and fabrics more easily than oil-based lubes. Oil-based lubricants can negatively affect the condom material and will stain fabric. Stains from water-based lubricants can be washed out.

Water-based lubricants are available in several general consistencies. Thin, almost like water, medium consistency (this is my preference), and thick like goo, or a thick sunblock. Thicker lubricants are said to be better for anal play since a thicker lubricant can create an extra cushion of comfort during anal sex and stay in place better.

However, I still prefer a medium consistency lubricant. As I stated earlier, I like a lubricant that is like a woman's own lubrication or slightly thicker, it enables you to feel more of her body texture. I also like that the medium consistency lubes because they provide a better slip and slide effect. Some of the thicker lubricants can be clumpy and/or stringy. Also, some lubricants dry flakier than others.

My preferences are the following lubricants with medium consistency:

1. **Please Liquid** – Glycerin free, great consistency, taste is decent to good. Not as good as a flavored lubricant, but good enough to lick for a long time. Con: when Please dries it is flaky. If you have dark bed covers or sheets and it gets on them, it will dry like a white flaky substance [**Image 4.22**].

Image 4.22

Chapter Four

2. <u>Sliquid-Sassy</u> – Glycerin free, great consistency, there is no taste so it does not taste bad [**Image 4.23**].

Image 4.23

3. **Astroglide** (with glycerin) – This is my **favorite**. I like the consistency, not too thick, and not too thin. You can feel every groove of her anatomy and she can feel every groove of you better than with silicone-based lubricants. It is not flaky and tastes fine. The glycerin free version does not taste good to me but try it. [**Image 4.24**].

Image 4.24

4. **ID Lube** (with glycerin) – Great consistency, tastes good, but make sure your partner is not prone to yeast infections if you use the glycerin types [**Image 4.25**].

Flavored lubricants are good for oral sex and are not recommended for vaginal intercourse or anal. The sugar content used to make them taste good could lead to yeast infections. They can be stickier because of sugar, and they are not recommended for anal, they tend not to last long enough. They are great if you are going to lick your partner for a long time on her vagina or her Gem, and if she is going to do the same to your penis, balls, and ass.

Image 4.25

If you are using a condom and you take it off for her to give you head, the flavored lubricant can help take away the taste of the condom. There are two types: 1. flavored with glycerin or 2. flavored with ingredients like aspartame and organic stevia. There are many different flavors, so the flavor choice is a preference decision.

My recommendation for flavored lubricants:

1. <u>Wet Flavored Intimacy Gel</u>
   Juicy Watermelon – sugar free and non staining [**Image 4.26**].

Image 4.26

2. <u>Sliquid Swirl</u> – Green Apple and Piña Colada [**See Image 4.27**].

Image 4.27

Update to lubes: New no glycerin or no sugar lubricants:

1. Aloe Cadabra – <u>Mango Passion Lube</u> for Anal Sex and Oral. This is a great new flavored option for oral sex but I did not think the lubrication lasted as long as Astroglide or LubeLife-Ana (below) for anal sex, though try for yourself. You can still use it for oral because it does taste good. Pina Colada this product is #5 in lubricants on Amazon. Great taste! You won't regret buying if you like Pina Coladas. No parabens, petroleum, glycerin, and glycol for both of the above lubes.

2. Lube Life – <u>Original</u> is the #1 lubricant on Amazon. The Original has a good consistency, it is slightly thinner than Astroglide, because it has no glycerin the taste is not as good. The <u>Anal Lubricant</u> has a thicker consistency that feels good (both the original and anal lube have no glycerin). There is also Watermelon flavored Watermelon and Strawberry Strawberry No sugar but have glycerin. You get more lube for your buck with these bottles but the dispenser is too big and not sexy during the act of sex. The lube dispenses well with the bottle I suggest below.

3. Lynk Pleasure – <u>Anal Lube</u>. The consistency is good but to me the flavor is not as good a Astroglide. Also, the pump bottle is not as easy to manage as the smaller bottle. I do like that you get more. I would recommend getting a different dispenser. I provided a link to a cool looking pump bottle below.

Below are different types of lubes based on the thickness of consistency and what I think of them. You can try them if my recommendation is not a product that you enjoy.

Thick water-based lubricants:

1. **Astroglide** – <u>Gel</u> I don't like thicker lubes for anal sex; the consistency does not provide a good slippery feel. Thicker than Please Liquid.

2. **Slippery Stuff** – <u>Gel</u> glycerin free and about the same consistency as Astroglide Gel, but it can be stringy.

Medium consistency water-based lubricants:

1. **Astroglide** – <u>Natural Feel</u>, glycerin- and paraben-free—nice consistency but I do not like the taste. You can taste for yourself at a Good Vibrations or by sample pack from a local sex store.

2. **Sliquid** – <u>Organics Natural</u> glycerin and paraben free. A decent lubricant, but I still prefer the consistency of Astroglide regular.

Thin water-based lubricants:

1. <u>**Sliquid H2O**</u> – Thin consistency and tastes okay.

2. <u>**Pink Water**</u> – Even thinner consistency, I did not like the taste.

Her Ulitmate Pleasure

Here is a **lube container** that looks smooth and is easy to hold with one hand and dispenses lube well.

A special note on silicon lubricants for anal sex: Some people online mention that they use silicone lube for anal sex and recommend it. For the introduction phase, I still recommend a water-based lubricant because you can feel more with it. Reapplying the lubricant frequently is also soothing to her gem during the beginning phase. You can test it for yourself; buy a silicone lube and a water-based lube and see which provides more sensation. After you enjoy anal sex frequently, you can see which you would like to use long-term. I still prefer water-based lube because I like the way it feels. I would love your feedback on your experience. Go to the Resources section to learn how to provide your One of the tools that can be used to lubricate her gem for anal sex is an **Anal Lube Shooter** [Image 4.28]. This will enable you to make sure she is well lubricated throughout her anal canal.

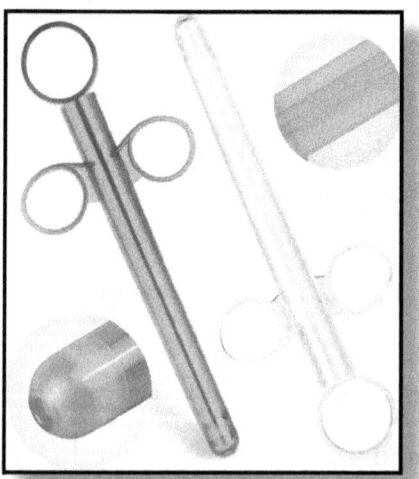

Image 4.28

You can also use **Balneol Hygienic Cleansing Lotion** to clean after anal sex. It is soothing and meant for genital cleansing [Image 4.29]. Use an "Adult Toy Cleaner/ Cleanser" to clean your toys before and after use. Now that you know some techniques on how to make anal play good, clean, and fun, you can enjoy the content of Chapters 3 and 5.

Image 4.29

Chapter Four

If you have toys that you love. I would like to learn about them. Send me an email to share the toys that drive you wild! EroticFlow.com is working on working on a toy. If you would like to be a beta user to provide feedback send me an email at David@EroticFlow.com. When the toy is in prototype I will send it to you for free to try out.

Chapter Summary

Chapter Four ~ Preparing for Pleasure

Making Anal Play Good Clean Fun

4.1 Hygiene

Making the pleasure zones delicious and safe for ultimate delight

a. Address the concern of cleanliness of anal play by having a fun and sensual way to clean her and you before you play.

b. Take a shower together, create the mood in the shower, light some candles, play some music (you can find good erotic music on Youtube.com/eroticflow/playlists), and sensually clean her body and her gem. If you're only up to Night 2, clean on the outside and the center of her gem only. Slide ¼-inch of your fingertip in her gem to clean it, so you are good when you lick her. Tell her you want to lick her really thoroughly and want both of you to be really clean.

c. Once you complete Night 3, go in with a lightly soapy little finger to wash the inside of her gem. Rinse her really well with water to make sure all the soap is gone.

d. Once you have completed Night 4, you can go in deeper with your middle finger and do as item (c.) above.

e. You should shave and wash yourself properly if you want her to massage or lick you. It is only fair that you make it a nice experience for her. You would not want to lick a hairy ass, so don't make her do it. There is more of a chance for things to stay around on hair.

f. Make sure you and she smell good; use a lotion or oil that leaves you smelling really good. Great products for smelling good are available on EroticFlow.com for a discount.

g. Cleaning system

   i. Use glycerin suppositories (you can get these at any drug store); don't leave the house until you get the urge to go to the bathroom.

   ii. After the suppository use an anal douche. Hold it in for as long as you can. Do this step twice.

   iii. Then use unscented baby wipes to clean deeply.

   iv. Take a shower, use a cleanser on the area and your gem, rinse well using your finger, then you are good to go.

   v. If some time passes before you actually start the fun, do a swipe with a baby wipe to make sure you are okay.

h. Get well educated on anal sex health, go to the Resources section.

i. It is vital to repeat a very important point that is clearly made in all the books on anal play, and that is you should not go from playing in her gem directly to her vagina with anything—fingers, toys, or your penis. You should not finger her gem and then play with her clitoris or on the outside her vagina with that finger because there's a chance you can give her a UTI if you play on top of the area of her urinary opening.

4.4 Toys for explosive anal orgasms
Making the process completely pleasurable

a. Get the right toys to make anal sexuality (anal play & sex) extremely pleasurable and a painless process.

b. You'll need two types of toys: toy/s for her clitoris and vagina, and toys for her gem.

c. The toys for her gem need a safety system so that they cannot be lost in the gem. There will be some sort of stopper or string that goes around your wrist.

d. Use vibrating plugs and the Berman Dilator when beginning to pleasure her gem. You can also use the other toys suggested for a variety of different pleasures.

e. You can use the Slim Vibe or a Clitoris and G-spot vibe for pleasuring her clitoris and vagina.

f. Minimum set is a small vibrating plug, the Berman set, a vibrating penis ring, and a slim vibe.

g. Always wash the toys with cleanser before and after play.

4.5 Lubricants
Enabling wetness to take her to new worlds of pleasure

a. Using a good lubricant is imperative to anal play and to getting her to enjoy the process.

b. The right consistency is important. Also, find out if she is allergic to sugars. You need to know this in case a lube with no glycerin or PABA is needed.

c. After testing and tasting a wide variety of lubricants, my favorite is an industry champion, Astroglide.

d. If she is not allergic to glycerin, you can use flavored lubricants on her and yourself to enjoy gem licking.

One of the tools to lubricate her gem for anal sex is an **Anal Lube Shooter**.

You can also use **Balneol Hygienic Cleansing Lotion** to clean after anal sex. It is soothing and meant for genital cleansing. Use an "Adult Toy Cleaner/Cleanser" to wash toys. Visit EroticFlow.com for where to buy. Now that you know some techniques on how to make anal play good, clean, and fun, enjoy the chapter to come; it will provide lots of pleasure to you and your lover.

Chapter Four

A special note on silicon lubricants for anal sex: Some people online mention that they use silicone lube for anal sex and recommend it. For the introduction phase, I still recommend a water-based lubricant because you can feel more with it. Reapplying the lubricant frequently is also soothing to her gem during the beginning phase. You can test it for yourself; buy a silicone lube and a water-based lube and see which provides more sensation. After you enjoy anal sex frequently, you can see which you would like to use long-term. I still prefer water-based lube because I like the way it feels. I would love your feedback on your experience. Go to the Resources section to learn how to provide your feedback and get rewarded.

Chapter Five
Erotic Anal Play

Delicious Stimulation for Both of You

5.1 Erotic AZ Play and Advanced Positions

Now that she is enjoying anal sexuality, you two can begin to diversify your newfound delight. In the following pages, I provide anal play techniques and positions, fun from A to Z. Toys are also incorporated to heighten pleasure for both of you. Stimulating multiple erogenous zones simultaneously to make her feel incredible will be covered. Include passionate, hot, erotic talk before, during, and after sex sessions. Find the exact words and phrases that turn both of you on. For couples that do not engage in erotic sex talk, sexuality is stimulation of all the senses, including what you both hear. Words are powerful aphrodisiacs. Therefore, if you don't, start light with Mmmms, YES, moans, groans, that feels sooo good, I love that, and gradually escalate over time to increase variety and more provocative terms and phrases. Remember, variety leads to more orgasmic experiences.

Women, enjoy the process of giving and receiving pleasure with the way you move, your moans, your words, facial expressions, and your flow with your lover. Men, pay special attention to the details provided for finger stimulation techniques and creating an emotional connection. Both of you should view it as a mutual work of art. Every time you engage, you are going to create a beautiful masterpiece of emotions, passion, creative variety, and erotic ecstasy.

Chapter Five

a. The E3

The E3 is about stimulating three erogenous areas at the same time, her clitoris, inside her vagina, and her gem. Place two small lubricant bottles next to you, one is for backup in case you can't easily reach the other. Have her lay on her back in the middle of the bed, use at least a full-size bed. Position yourself somewhat perpendicular to her while laying sideways on your left side (for a right-handed person) [See **Figure 5.1**].

Pour lubricant on your hands, her clitoris, vagina, and gem. Arouse her first, use the head of your penis to play with her clitoris, her lips, and around her gem. Now lift her ass so that your left-hand with lubricated fingers can play with her gem, while your right hand focuses on stimulating her clitoris and her vagina [See **Figure 5.2**].

Figure 5.1

Now, you'll slide your penis in her vagina. Start thrusting inside of her, waving your body, circling your hips, going in and out while you are simultaneously stimulating her clitoris, vagina, and gem. Sensually enter her gem with the middle finger of your left hand and go in slowly. Enter as deep as possible and make sure it is comfortable for her.

Creatively stimulate her gem, clitoris, and vagina. She can reach down and put her hands on your ass to pull you in deeper. Now she can enjoy you thrusting inside her vagina with your penis, your right hand stimulating her clitoris and lips and your left-hand fingers inside her gem. All three will feel good to her.

Figure 5.2

After she is accustomed to one finger in her gem, slide two fingers into her gem using the same technique [**See Figure 5.3**]. A variation of E3 is once she is enjoying anal sex, slide your penis into her gem, and use one hand to massage her G-spot with you middle, and ring fingers while you massage her clitoris with your thumb. With your other hand, massage around her gem ring sensually as you slide your penis in and out of her gem.

Figure 5.3

Chapter Five

b. Palms of Pleasure

In this position, you will play with her beautiful vagina while you go inside her gem in a reverse cowgirl position. The important part is the finger stimulation technique to her vagina and around her gem.

Lubricate your penis, pelvic area, all over her gem, and vagina. Slide your penis in her gem in the reverse cowgirl position.

Right hand:

1. Insert your middle and ring fingers into her vagina. Curl your fingers so that they massage her G-spot and use your palm to stimulate her lubricated clitoris and U-spot. Massage her clitoris with your palm sensually as you go in and out of her vagina with your fingers.

2. Use your first finger and little fingers to massage her labia as you go in and out of her vagina.

Left hand:

1. Use your first and middle fingers to massage her gem ring and her tang.

2. Use your ring and little fingers to massage the backside of her gem ring.

Lick and bite her shoulders. Imagine that you are sending your erotic energy to your palm, fingers, and penis. Keep massaging her clitoris and U-spot in circles, side to side, up and down, and faster and slower and in sync with the rhythm of the music you are listening to. Ask her what movement she likes the most and have her play with her

Figure 5.4

clitoris as well, and she will probably have an incredible orgasm squeezing her gem around your penis [See Figure 5.4].

You can also use your right hand's fingers and palm to stimulate her clitoris and labia while your left fingers goes into her vagina as far as possible to stimulate her G-spot and perineal sponge. You will be able to reach further with your left hand. If you do both techniques, sequence your left-hand fingers in her vagina first before massing around her gem for her optimal safety.

Palms of Pleasure Variation: have her lay down on her back along the edge of the bed. You are not going to enter her with your penis on this one; you'll just stand on the side of the bed, and use your hands to stimulate her. Lubricate her well. Use one hand for palm-massaging her clitoris and insert your middle and ring fingers into her vagina, massage her G-spot, and come back to play with U-spot. Now use your other hand to insert two fingers into her gem, your first finger on top of your middle finger or middle and third finger side by side. Use your thumb to massage her tang as you go in and out of her gem

c. The V-Spot Massage

This licking technique is VERY pleasurable for your partner. I call it the **V-Spot Massage** because you will be massaging her vagina from the bottom up in a V-type movement "v", and from top-down in an upside-down V movement "^". Some fun multi-tasking to enjoy. The V-Spot licking technique starts by lubing her gem, vagina, clitoris, and all around her labia. I'll describe the act for a right-hand person. Use your dominant hand on the bottom. Lay her on the edge of your bed so you have room to move around and have leverage when standing or kneeling on the floor [See Figure 5.5].

1. Insert your ring finger into her gem using circling. After doing the V-Spot massage for a little while, you can also insert your little finger at the same time.

2. Insert your middle finger into her vagina and massage her G-spot and perineal sponge.

Chapter Five

3. Use your thumb and first finger to massage her labia and surrounding area creating a V-shaped motion.

4. Take your other hand and do a similar action, coming down from the top of her clitoris to both sides of her vagina. Play with her clitoris, and massage it with your thumb and finger like you are stroking her off.

5. Lick, suck, and kiss her clitoris, her vagina, labia, and her legs while you are doing

Figure 5.5

the finger technique described above [See Figure 5.6]. Sensually massage her labia and clitoris into your lips; suck and lick her with all your passion.

6. Move your right hand in and out so your ring finger is going in and out of her gem while your other fingers are massaging her vagina.

7. Tell her how beautiful she tastes, feels, and looks. Talk dirty, hum and moan passionately on her clitoris and vagina to create subtle vibrations with your tongue and lips.

Switch stimulation by moving your top hand to stimulate her nipples. Kiss and lick her stomach while your bottom hand is still moving back and forth. Do so sensually, passionately, and vary the intensity. Use your

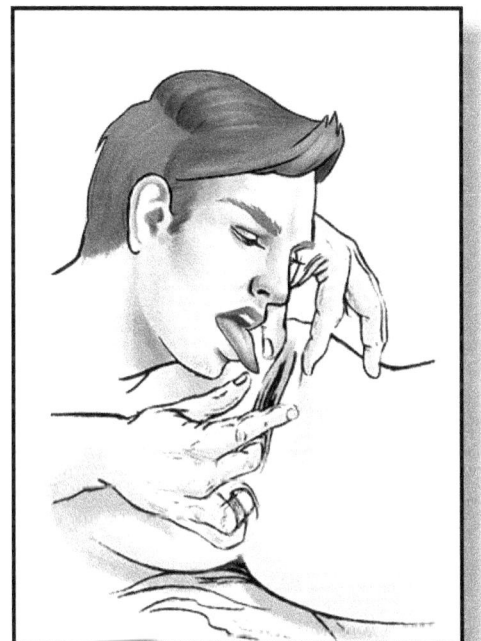

Figure 5.6

first finger from the bottom hand to stimulate her clitoris while your other hand is on her breasts and nipples and your mouth is going to multiple erogenous zones and back to her clitoris.

d. The V-Spot Massage and Vibe Combo

The V-Spot massage helps her adjust for a bigger girth inside her gem. You are going to use a vibrator or the Vibrating Plug in her gem while doing the V-Spot massage covered above.

1. Insert the Vibrating Plug and hold it with your little and ring fingers. Circle the toy into her gem, slowly and sensually. Use your fingers to guide the vibrating plug back and forth. Alternatively, you can use one of the vibes from the Berman Dilator Set. Attach the first or second additional attachment to the base toy [**See Figure 5.7**].

2. Insert the middle finger of the same hand into her vagina, and massage her perineal sponge.

3. Use your thumb and first finger to massage the sides of her vagina and her lips.

4. Use your other hand's thumb and fingers to massage her clitoris. Implement all the other aspects of the V-Spot massage.

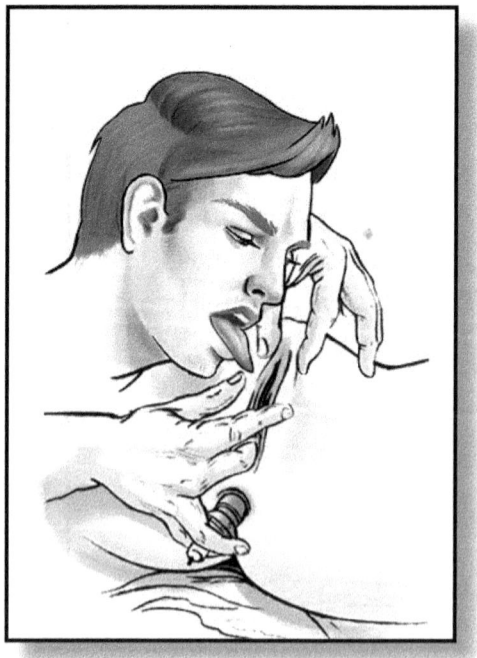

Figure 5.7

Chapter Five

e. Missionary Work

It's all about giving

Figure 5.8

While you are in a missionary position as you are going into her gem, reach around with one or both hands and massage the area around her gem sensually.

Left or right hand:

1. Use your first finger to massage the back of her gem ring.

2. Your middle finger massages the area in between her gem and her vagina, the tang area.

3. The ring finger plays with her clitoris. Then kiss her passionately, bite into her neck as you slide in and out of her gem.

4. Use your fingers to massage all around her gem. Synchronize the massage of your fingers with your strokes into her gem. As you slide your middle finger across her tang, thrust deep inside of her gem.

5. Use your other hand to stimulate her in other erogenous zones.

This technique heightens intimacy because your heart is next to hers. It enhances emotional connection during anal sex especially as you kiss passionately [See **Figure 5.8**].

Also, during vaginal **missionary work,** reach around to massage all the areas mentioned above.

Left or right hand:

1. Insert your first finger into her gem.

2. Your middle finger plays with her tang.

3. Your ring finger is on the other side of your penis, playing with her clitoris as you are thrusting in and out of her vagina.

Figure 5.9

You can also insert two or more fingers inside her gem. [**See Figure 5.9**]. Also insert a toy into her gem in this position, a plug, Berman dilator, or the Couples Dual Motor Vibrator (insert the big end into her gem and the small end in her vagina or facing her butt upward).

f. Tongue Tingle

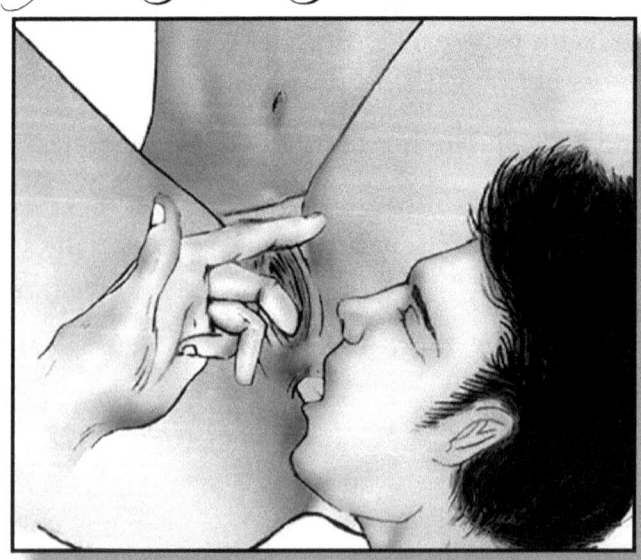

Figure 5.10

Lay her on her back and lick her gem. Make sure you penetrate it with your tongue as much as you can, slowly. Once you enter as deep as you can, curve your tongue up. Now insert your middle finger into her vagina. Curve the finger

Chapter Five

down so that you can massage your tongue through her gem. Circle your finger(s) around your tongue. Massage it in many ways, and then exchange your finger for a toy and massage your tongue with the toy. Curve down the vibrating toy to vibrate your tongue and to massage her G-spot [See **Figure 5.10**].

g. Pleasure Twists

This technique is important during the introduction phase and is very pleasurable for ongoing anal sex.

1. As you start to put the head of your penis inside her gem, use your dominant hand and put your fingers around the head. Make sure they are all well lubricated. Sensually twist your fingers around the head of your penis so the side of your first finger to the bottom of your thumb can massage the area around her gem.

2. Insert your thumb into her vagina. As you twist your fingers around, your thumb slides in and out of her vagina, massaging her tang and perineal sponge.

3. As you are doing this, grab your shaft and enter her slowly, use Circling and My Vibe techniques (covered in Night 6) to get her adjusted to your width. Keep massaging and twisting your fingers around her anal ring as you thrust back and forth in her gem deeply.

4. Take your other hand and massage her clitoris or nipples, switch back and forth.

5. Pull up, move side to side, and wave your body inside her gem while doing all the above.

It is important to master this technique. It will enable significant anal pleasure during penetration. Find out what amount of pressure she likes for the massage movements [See **Figure 5.11**].

Her Ultimate Pleasure

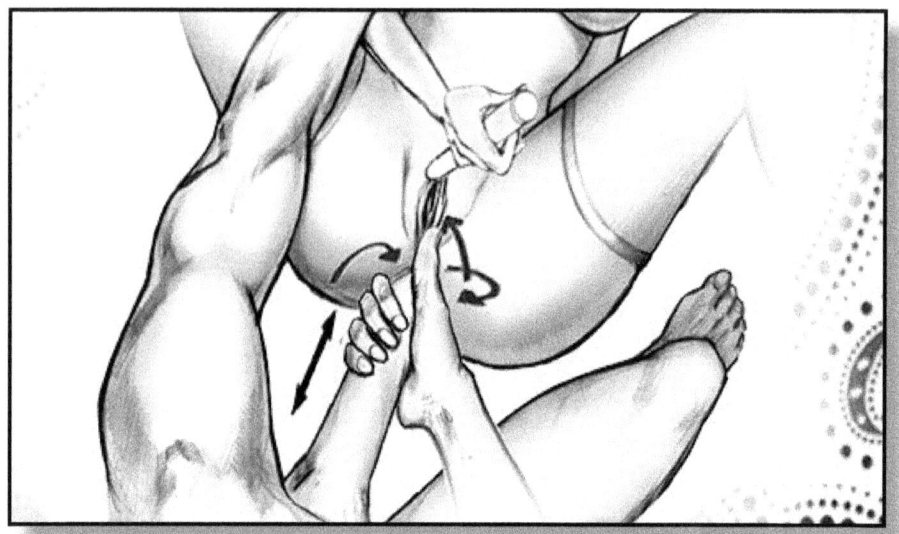

Figure 5.11

You can use the Couple Vibrator with Dural Motors for clitoral and G-spot stimulation. Insert the small end into her vagina to stimulate her G-spot; you might have to hold it in place with one hand, although it might stay in on its own. Another method for using the toy is to insert the big side into her vagina to stimulate her G-spot while the small side vibrates her clitoris. This method tends to keep the toy from moving around.

h. *The CrissCross*

Get into a 69 position, with you at the bottom. Lick her thighs sensually from one thigh across her vagina to her other thigh. Kiss her clitoris sensually and passionately. Now you are going to insert the middle finger of your left hand into her vagina and the middle finger of your right hand into her gem. Move your fingers in and out while making a circular massaging motion with your fingers. The left-hand middle finger will be massaging her G-spot.

Now, you are going to start sucking her clitoris, wrapping your lips around with the tip of your tongue waving and massaging the tip of her clitoris. Feel all your energy come to your mouth, lips, and tongue. Feel your heart and soul concentrated on her clitoris. As you do this, you are going to pull down the finger that is inserted in her gem and push up the finger

Chapter Five

that is in her vagina. You'll feel like your fingers are crisscrossing [**See Figure 5.12**].

Slightly wave your fingers; move them to the Crisscross position slowly to make sure she is enjoying the process. Moan on her clitoris so that your throat creates vibrations that resonate onto her lips and clitoris. What you two hear is very stimulating; give her ear candy while you are sucking her.

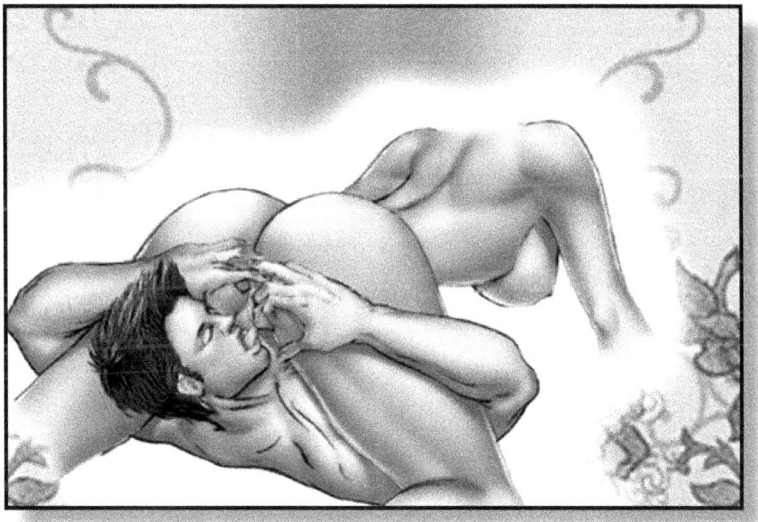

Figure 5.12

i. *The Straddle and Flip*

While you are on your back at the top of the bed, have her straddle your face with her hands on the wall or on the bed frame. Her clitoris and lips are over your mouth. Start by kissing, licking, and biting her inner thighs. Keep circling your tongue and take light to deep sensual bites of her as you work your way towards her center. As you get close to her lips, slow down and glide your tongue across her lips lightly. Make sure your tongue is really wet, and make your tongue warmer by breathing warm breaths into your mouth.

After pleasuring her clitoris and vagina, have her tilt her gem to your mouth so you can lick it sensually and passionately [**See Figure 5.13**].

Her Ultimate Pleasure

Figure 5.13

Enjoy her soft gem over your tongue. Have her spread her knees so more of her gem is flushed up against your tongue and her wetness is all over you. Then put your hands on her torso and push her back so she rolls back on the bed onto her shoulders and her ass rolls up to face the ceiling. At the same time, you scoot backward, so your that back is to the bed frame or wall **(the move in 5.14 is a transition to 5.15)** [See Figures 5.14 & 5.15].

Her shoulders and upper back are on the bed, her knees are by her shoulders, and her lower back is going to lay against your torso. Your legs are spread to give her room to lie in between, and you are sitting upright. In this position, you have full access to her gem and vagina in a very hot position.

Begin to lick her softly and build up the passion. Lick her vagina and her clitoris. Then lick her gem while you massage her clitoris with your fingers.

Figure 5.14

Right hand:

1. Your first finger massages the backside of her gem while you lick her gem.

Chapter Five

2. Your middle finger massages the inner ring of her gem. Your ring finger massages her tang and the bottom of her vagina.

3. Your little finger massages the labia.

Left hand:

1. Your first finger massages around your tongue while licking her gem.

2. Your middle and ring fingers massage her vagina, G-spot, and perineal sponge.

Figure 5.15

3. Your little finger massages her clitoris [**See Figure 5.15**].

You can add toys to this play. Use one hand to hold the toy and play with her clitoris and the inside of her vagina. Use the side of your hand to twist the toy and massage her labia and clitoris. Use your other hand to spread her ass cheeks apart and lick her gem as deeply as you can. Ask her to spread her ass with her hands so you can lick her gem even deeper [See Figure 5.16]. Use two toys, one to stimulate her clitoris and another in her vagina while you lick her gem.

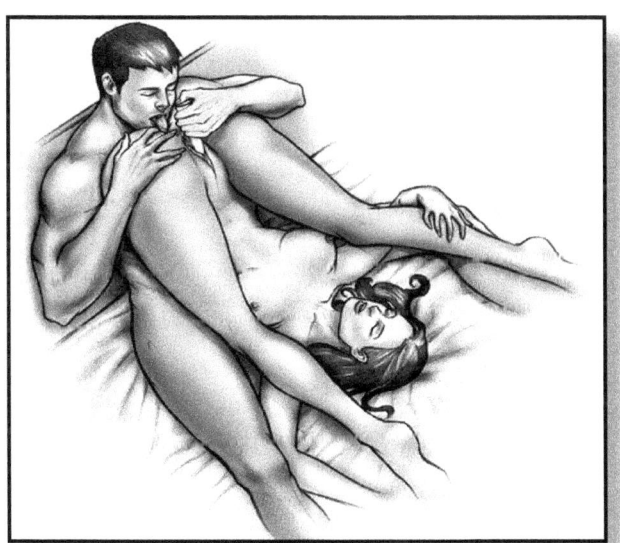

Figure 5.16

Then, you can insert a third toy into her gem while she holds the toy vibrating her clitoris.

Good Vibes

This is one of my favorite anal play positions with a toy. Once your partner likes anal toy play, you can engage in this act. After you have warmed her up for anal play, get a chair, preferably an office chair that drops low, swivels around, and has no arms. Drop the chair to its lowest position. Have her straddle you and enter her vagina. Use the head of your penis to play with her vagina before you enter. Use a vibrator with either a flared baser or another system to ensure the vibrator does not go all the way in.

Lubricate her gem, the vibrator, her clitoris, and your pelvic area so her clitoris slides on you when she rides you. First, play with the tip of the vibrator on her gem. Then slowly start to insert the vibrator in her gem. Once the vibrator is inside, hold it still for a little bit so you both feel the vibrations. You'll feel the vibrations through the thin wall between her ass and vagina. It will feel incredible for both of you! Go in and out, then in circles with the vibe. By tilting the back of the vibe up, you'll angle to the front towards your penis. This is the definition of good vibrations. Mmmm, mmmm, good vibes! Use your fingers to add stimulation:

Right hand:

1. Your first finger massages the backside of her gem ring around the vibrator.

2. Your middle finger massages the front side gem ring.

3. Your ring finger massages the tang.

4. Your little finger massages her clitoris. You can also do this with your ring finger.

Left hand:

1. Hold the vibrator while circling it and twisting it.

Chapter Five

2. Use the side of your hand that is against her skin to massage her gem ring by twisting the vibrator when it is deeper inside her gem [**See Figure 5.17**].

Both of you will most likely explode from this play. You can also switch to sliding your penis in her gem and use a cleaned Vibrating Plug in her vagina. Position the plug stopper vertically on top of her clitoris so that it is more stimulating for her clitoris or horizontally if it is more comfortable. After the plug is comfortably in her vagina, you can enter her gem and enjoy. You can also use the couple clitoris and G-spot vibrator for this position.

Figure 5.17

Another way to add good vibes, is to put on a vibrating penis ring. While you are in her vagina, it will add vibrations to her clitoris and you'll feel vibrations from the ring and the toy in her gem. It feels good!

k. Pearls

After she has been thoroughly stimulated from both regular sex and anal play, and just before she has an orgasm, use a pearl necklace or silicone beads to massage her ass. Now push the pearls into her gem. Get pearls in a couple of different sizes to see which ones she likes best.

Put in as many as you can as long as she feels comfortable, then continue to have sex. Have her tell you when she is about to orgasm so you can pull out all the pearls as she is having an explosive orgasm. Pull them out at a speed that will enable her to enjoy the grooves of the pearls coming out of her gem. Not too fast. Ask her afterward what speed she likes so

Her Ultimate Pleasure

you know exactly how to make it feel best for her. Always clean your toys thoroughly after play. To cleanse the pearls for use at another time, put them into boiling water. To make sure the pearl string doesn't break easily, test its strength before you insert it into her [**See Figure 5.18**].

Figure 5.18

l. Fingertips

During this type of anal play, you'll want her on her back. You are going to arouse her as usual. After some finger play, you are going to lick her vagina and clitoris. Then slowly guide your middle finger into her gem or you can slide both first and middle fingers inside. Make sure your fingers are clean and well filed for all anal insertion activities.

Next, sensually guide your thumb into her vagina. Touch the fingertip of your thumb to your middle finger inside her gem. Massage your fingers in circles, side to side, and in and out. Continue to lick her clitoris at the same time. Use your other hand to stimulate both of her nipples. Have her lick your fingers to get them wet and ready for touching and playing with her nipples.

You can also pull out your thumb and insert two fingers from your other hand into her vagina. Turn them over horizontally to play with and massage the finger or fingers in her gem. Massage back and forth, side to side, shake, and jiggle. Trace the outlines of your fingers massaging her inner

Chapter Five

Figure 5.19

sugar walls [**See Figure 5.19**]. This technique stimulates the perineal sponge that will enhance pleasure.

m. *Eyes Wide Shut*

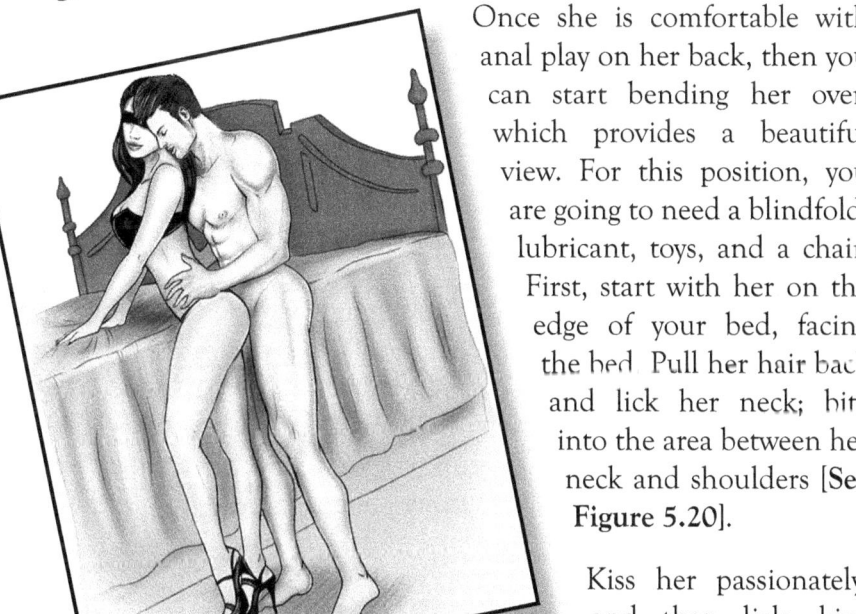

Figure 5.20

Once she is comfortable with anal play on her back, then you can start bending her over, which provides a beautiful view. For this position, you are going to need a blindfold, lubricant, toys, and a chair. First, start with her on the edge of your bed, facing the bed. Pull her hair back and lick her neck; bite into the area between her neck and shoulders [**See Figure 5.20**].

Kiss her passionately, and then lick, kiss, and bite the back of her neck. Now will blindfold her, heightening her other senses. Continue to lick her back, shoulders, and circle your tongue down to her lower back [See Figure 5.21].

Stay there for a bit, and then continue down to her ass cheeks, take soft, sensuous bites of her cheeks. Continue down the back of her leg, then to the back of her calves, and down to her ankles. Come back up and over her inner thighs, and lick across her wetness. Go down the other leg and repeat this process. Arouse her until she is dripping onto your tongue.

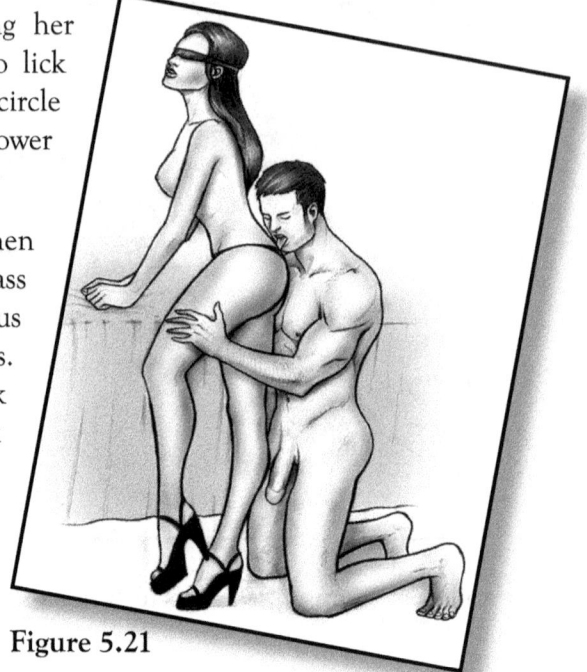

Figure 5.21

Get her to kneel on the bed on all fours. Have her put her head down towards the bed and arch her back so that her ass is angled upward as much as possible. Pull up the chair to the edge of the bed because you are going to be here a while, fully indulging in the beauty of her ass, vagina, and gem [See Figure 5.22].

Start to lick her cheeks, kissing and lightly biting them, then lick the area around her gem.

Let your breath warm her gem. Take a light lick of her gem from bottom to top, then from the top, do circles on her gem down to her clitoris. Circle there and suck her lips as you come back to her gem. Take both hands and gently squeeze her ass. Then spread her ass cheeks to fully expose her gem so you can pleasure it thoroughly. Start to lick her gem, slowly at first, letting the warmth of your breath onto it, and then more passionately.

Have her reach back to spread her ass cheeks for you so that she can join the erotic play. This frees your hands up to start playing with her vagina. Gently circle and slowly slide your warm tongue into her gem. Sensually

Chapter Five

go as deep as you can while she spreads her ass cheeks for you.

Meanwhile, play with her clitoris. You can also slide two fingers into her vagina and slide the vibrator into her gem. Now she is bent over with the triple stimulation of your tongue around her gem ring while a vibrator is inside, your fingers are in her vagina, and you're playing with her clitoris.

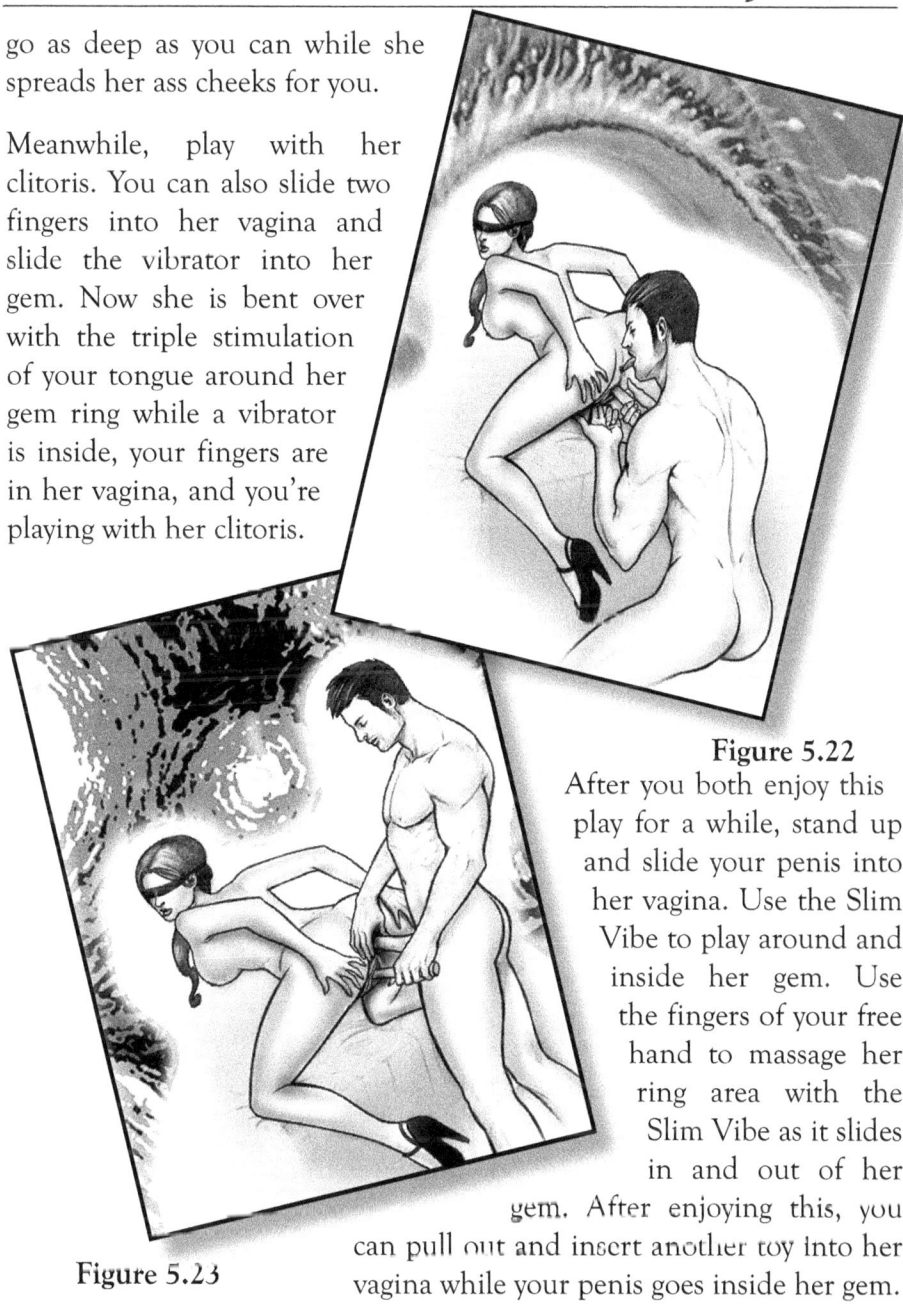

Figure 5.22
After you both enjoy this play for a while, stand up and slide your penis into her vagina. Use the Slim Vibe to play around and inside her gem. Use the fingers of your free hand to massage her ring area with the Slim Vibe as it slides in and out of her gem. After enjoying this, you can pull out and insert another toy into her vagina while your penis goes inside her gem.

Figure 5.23

Now use the fingers of your free hand to massage her ring area around your penis, sliding in and out of her gem [See **Figure 5.23**].

Continue to use a variety of toys to stimulate her. Remember to lubricate these toys, and not to go from her gem to her vagina with these toys. This position is delightful to look at. You can let her enjoy the vision by taking a picture or a video from your perspective and showing it to her later. She can delete it afterward if she wants, but it is a great way to share your visual experience with her.

n. Upside Down Gem Spot

This position is famous in the adult film industry. I am going to add some technique to what you have probably already seen. This is a very visually stimulating position for both of you. You can do this position at the edge of the bed or the couch. You should have toys, a lubricant, and extra-soft pillows.

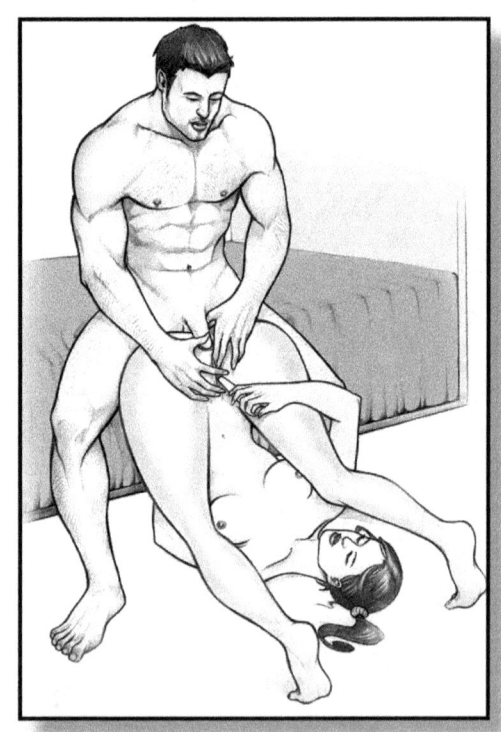

There are several ways to enter and perform this position. First, we will start with the bed method. Put several pillows on the floor near the edge of the bed. Sit on the edge of the bed, and have her straddle you with her legs extended out on the bed. Lean her back, support her back with your arms. Let her head drop until her shoulders land on top of the pillows on the floor [**See Figure 5.24**].

Make sure she is comfortable. Play with her clitoris, vagina, and gem with the head of your penis. Get her really wet and lubricate her gem. You can

Figure 5.24

now enter her gem slowly. Use a vibrator on her clitoris as you enter. You are now standing over her gem in a slightly crouched position. First, enjoy going up and down in this position.

Right hand:

1. Middle and ring fingers on her clitoris.

Chapter Five

2. First finger stimulates her vaginal lips and inside her vagina.

3. Thumb massages the circumference of her gem.

Left hand:

1. First, and middle fingers massage her tang.

2. Thumb massages circumference of gem on backside of your penis.

3. Ring finger on her labia.

Figure 5.25

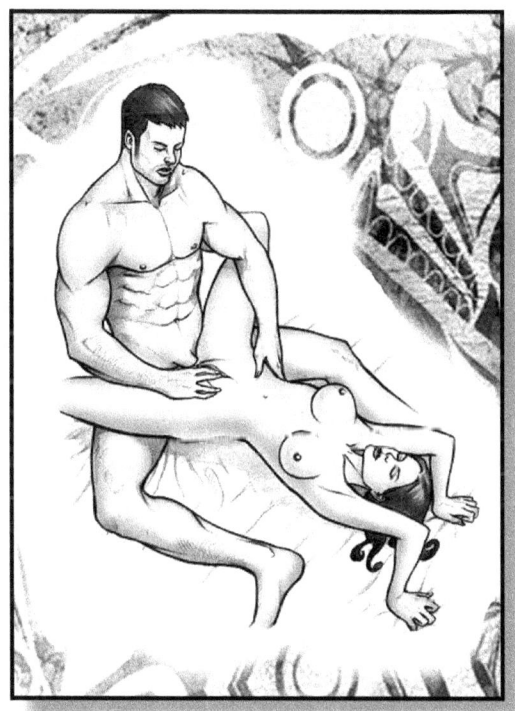

Figure 5.26

Lean back to angle the head of your penis toward her G-spot through her ass. You might need to slide the top mattress back somewhat from the box spring so it gives you room to move back and forth and down and around. You might need to push her slightly forward to get it right. Move up and down as well as back and forth to see what feels best to her. Make finding her G-spot fun. Once you find the area, move around to have your penis's head massage the spot sensually. Simultaneously play with her clitoris and vagina.

Pull out, and turn around to go in her gem with you facing the bed. Slap, jiggle, and massage her ass. Use your fingers to massage her gem ring as you slide in and out [**See Figure 5.25**].

Another variation of this position is for you to sit in the middle of the bed. Have her straddle you as you enter her gem and have her lean back on the bed. Use your fingers to massage her tang, vagina, and clitoris while you move back and forth in her gem [**See Figure 5.26**].

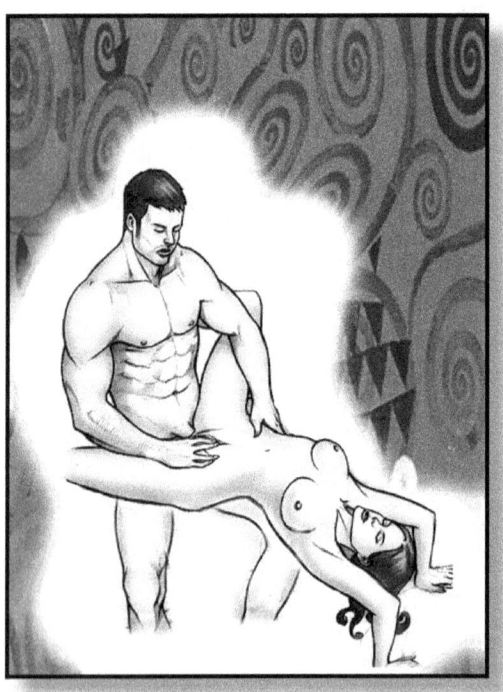

Figure 5.27

If you are feeling adventurous, you can get acrobatic with this position. Have her straddle you on the edge of the bed with her back turned away from the bed. Enter her gem, then have her wrap her legs around your back to secure herself and put your hands around her back. She'll lean back towards the floor and put her arms and hands back to the floor. Stand up and angle yourself to massage her G-spot with the head of your penis through her ass. Use your fingers to massage her tang, vagina, and clitoris [**See Figure 5.27**]. Also, use toys to stimulate the area.

o. *Gem 69*

You can do this while you are on her back with both of you on your sides or while she is on her back. Have toys and lubricant ready and nearby. You can both enjoy the pleasure provided by a warm, wet tongue on your gem. Make sure your hygiene preparation is as good as when she did it in

Chapter Five

order to make it pleasurable for her too. This means shaving your ass! She does not want to lick a really hairy ass.

More importantly, you will feel a lot more of her tongue when you are shaved. Here's advice from Manscaped.com on how to shave yourself. You should also clean up with antibacterial soap just like she does and with your finger going inside of you. Start by licking her vagina and move to include her ass. She starts at your penis, then to your balls, and licks until you both "end up" in gem 69. You can use toys to add to your pleasures.

p. Upside Down V-Lick

This is just like the V-Lick, but in this position, she'll be kneeling on the bed bent over with her head to the middle of the bed. Have her put her breasts as close to the bed and her ass up in the air as much as possible, so her gem is facing up. Next, she reaches back with both hands to grab each butt cheek and slowly spreads her gem for you to indulge in licking her.

After some erotic licking of her vagina and gem, slide your middle finger from your dominant hand into her vagina and curve it up toward her gem. Sensually slide your tongue deep into her gem so you can feel your finger inside her vagina. Use your finger to massage your tongue, her perineal sponge, and G-spot while you lick her gem.

Now, also insert your first finger along with your middle finger into her vagina. Curve both up with the soft side of your fingers facing toward your face. Spread your fingers to make a slight V-shape so she can feel your tongue in the middle of them. Pull your fingers back toward your mouth so that your tongue goes in even deeper and lick between the V created by your fingers. Massage your fingers with your tongue and your tongue with your fingers in a variety of ways. Move them back and forth along your tongue, this will help you stimulate her gem deeply.

You can now do a V-Spot massage. Lubricate her clitoris, vagina area, and gem area. Below is the description of the procedure for a dominantly right-handed individual.

Right hand:

1. Slide your ring finger into her gem while your middle finger goes into her vagina.

2. Extend your first finger and thumb to massage the sides of her vagina.

Left hand:

1. Use your first finger and thumb to massage her clitoris.

2. Switch to inserting your middle finger into her vagina along with your other middle finger; curve it to massage her G-spot. Use your palm to stimulate her clitoris as you slide your finger over and around her G-spot, also slide it in and out of her vagina. Switch back and forth between left hand step one and two.

You now have two hands at play with the back of your middle fingers facing one another. While your bottom hand's middle finger is in her vagina extend your first and ring fingers to massage the area around her tang and gem. Simultaneously, your mouth will go wherever it can find room to kiss, suck, bite, and lick her deliciously.

g. Ride-Em

Once your partner has gone through all 7 Nights and is comfortable with anal sex, you can do practically everything that is possible with vaginal sex (depending on your size and how comfortable it feels for her in different positions). Although, with anal sex, there are some interesting dynamics and angles that add pleasure in these positions. You may need a small pillow under your butt for the Ride-Em position depending on the firmness of your bed.

Prop your back against pillows to the headboard. Have her straddle you. Having an adjustable incline weight bench is also great for this position, but not necessary. Put lubricant all over her ass, vagina, clitoris, and the area above her clitoris. Then, put lubricant all over your penis, your balls, and your entire pelvic area so she slides easily on your pelvic bone to stimulate her clitoris.

Chapter Five

Enter her gem while massaging it as you go in. Have her lay her breasts on your chest. Her vagina and lips will now be placed flush against your pelvic bone area, and since you are in her gem, her clitoris will be higher and right around your pelvic bone. Since you both are fully lubed, have her slide up and slowly go down while gently moving her hips around. The slippery effect of the lubricant allows her to slide up and down easily.

Now, focus on having her clitoris slide up and down on your pelvic bone. Play with direction and tilt your pelvic bone higher to stimulate her. Try putting a small pillow under your ass and back to lift your pelvic area higher. Pour more lubricant on her gem. Use both hands to sensually massage her ass and her gem, which is wrapped around your penis. Play with her ass, massage it, squeeze it together, then spread it.

Shake each of her ass cheeks in opposite directions and in the same direction, fast and at varying speeds. The shaking creates vibration and adds stimulation. Add more lube and have your fingers trace the circle of her gem around your penis. This serves two purposes: First, it adds stimulation to her gem. Second, it keeps your penis and her gem well lubricated while you are sliding in, out, and all around. Reach around and use your fingers as follows:

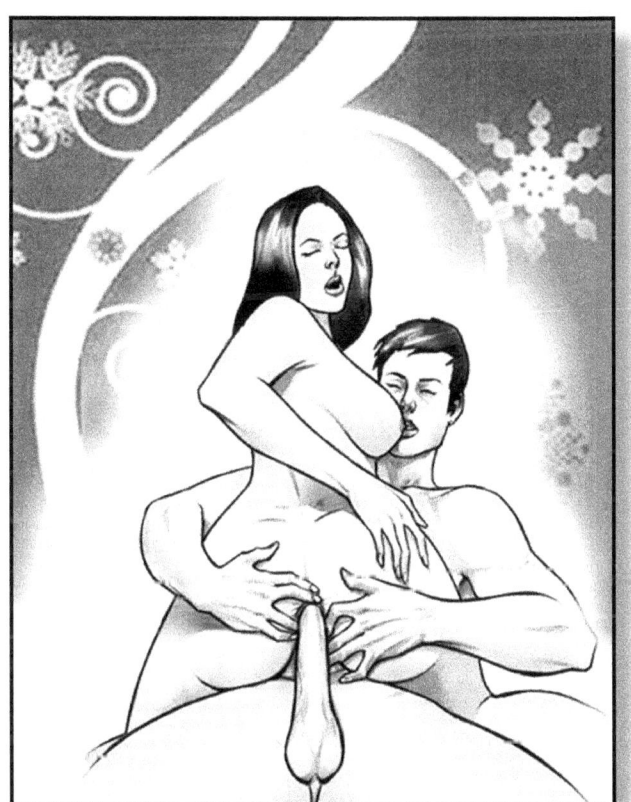

Figure 5.28

Right hand

1. Use your little and ring finger to massage and play with her gem ring and tang.

2. Use your first and middle fingers to massage the backside of her gem ring.

Left hand:

1. Use your first and middle fingers to massage the other side of her gem.

2. Use your ring and little fingers to massage her vagina and her clitoris (designate these fingers for vagina play only. Do not use the gem play fingers for playing with her vagina) [**See Figure 5.28**]. Wave your body to stimulate her G-spot. Enjoy!

You can also use the **Ride The Grooves** technique. Place your palm on your pelvic bone so the grooves of your knuckles are directly under her clitoris. Turn your hand so that the row of knuckles is in up and down alignment with her labia so when she moves back and forth, her clitoris rides the grooves of your knuckles. Lift your knuckles to adjust for her pleasure. You can also wave your knuckles to see how she likes the movement.

r. *Ride Him On All Fours*

Use a couch for this position. You lay on the floor with the back of your knees, calves, and feet on a couch. She'll then stand over you at the edge of the couch, while you face each other. Lift your butt up as high as possible, and she'll squat down so you slide in her gem. Then use the couch as leverage for your legs to thrust up. She'll put her hands on the couch for support and use the strength of her arms and legs to do squats up and down. She can squat to an ideal position so you can thrust up and down for her pleasure, and you can hold a level position so she can slide up and down for your pleasure. Use your fingers to add stimulation:

Right hand:

1. Use your thumb and/or fingers on her clitoris and U-spot. Also, use your thumb to play with her G-spot while your fingers play with her clitoris.

Left hand:

1.   Use your thumb to massage the ring of her gem and her tang.

Chapter Five

Figure 5.29

2. Use other fingers to play with her labia, the inside of her vagina, and her perineal sponge.

Regardless of who is moving, it's all pleasurable for both, and the view is delightful [**See Figure 5.29**].

5. G&G

G&G stands for gem and G-spot. Lay her on her back on the edge of your bed. You are going to be standing at the edge of the bed. Lubricate her gem, clitoris, and vagina. Use Pleasure Twists to enter her gem. Once you are in her gem, you're going to move to the side a bit so you can use your right hand for stroking your fingers in and out of her vagina.

Right hand:

1. Slide your middle finger (and first finger if she likes two fingers) into her vagina. Curve up your fingers to stimulate her G-spot.

Figure 5.30

2. Massage her U-spot and labia with your thumb.

Left hand:

1. Use your thumb and first finger to massage and stroke her clitoris.

2. Switch and use your middle and ring fingers to massage from the top of her clitoris down to her labia. Use the back of your fingers (the side with your fingers nails) to massage her, use knuckles as well for the sensation of groves.

Lick your left fingers, give her clitoris a light slap, and then massage it sensually. Add to the stimulation by using a toy, or she can hold the toy to stimulate her clitoris as you play with her nipples.

Massage her G-spot; imagine sending warm energy/heat to your fingers. Circle her G-spot and all around her vagina. You can also use a G-spot toy instead of your fingers. You have many options to stimulate these designated areas. This position provides a good view of your penis entering her beautiful gem, her wet sweet lips spread, and her aroused clitoris [**See Figure 5.30**]. Another way to stimulate her G-spot is to use a

Chapter Five

dual motor toy. Try the big motor in her vagina to stimulate her G-spot with the small motor on her clitoris; it tends to stay in place better.

Another stimulating option used in this position is to insert your thumb inside her vagina so the soft side is up. Massage her G-spot with your thumb and her clitoris with the palm area under your fingers.

You can also insert your penis into her vagina, but remember that if you have already been in her gem, you need to change condoms. Now use your fingers to play with her gem. It's just like Figure 5.30, except your penis will be in her vagina. Your left hand will be in the same position and the right hand will pleasure the gem in a couple of ways.

1. You can insert your middle finger into her gem, while your thumb plays with her U-spot.

2. You can insert two or more fingers into her gem deeply, while your thumb plays with the area between your penis and her gem. She'll enjoy the double penetration from the heat of your hands and your penis. You both will probably orgasm from how good this feels.

Another way to angle your penis to massage her G-spot through her gem is to position her gem at the edge of the bed instead of moving back and forth in her gem. Let your knees drop down so your penis is angled directly up and will be massaging her G-spot on the way back up. Keep moving down and back up. Also, do this movement when you are in her vagina. While in her vagina, if you put a pillow below her ass, you can angle yourself to reach her cul-de-sac, an arousal zone illustrated in Figure 3.12. Experiment with different angles to reach and stimulate the cul-de-sac; it can provide lots of pleasure for her.

t. Reverse Cowgirl Massage

In this reverse cowgirl position, both hands are going to come from under her ass to give her pleasure, as she rides your penis with her gem. She'll lie back on your chest. You are going to reach around with both hands.

Right hand:

1. Put the first and middle fingers across and above her gem to massage her tang.

Figure 5.31

2. The ring finger and little finger go below your penis to massage the backside gem area.

Left hand:

1. Use your ring finger and little finger to play with the inside of her vagina.

2. Use your first and middle fingers to massage her clitoris.

Massage your fingers across her tang as you thrust deep in her gem. Do not switch hands once you have started. Keep the gem massage hand on the gem area and the vagina massage hand on the vagina [See Figure 5.31].

u. Bend Over, Beautiful

A favorite position in anal sex is the doggy-style position. There are many ways to add stimulation to this position. Slide your penis into her vagina. Insert your middle finger inside her gem (you can also insert your first finger) depending on what turns her on. Curve your finger(s) down so that you are applying pressure on top of your penis pushing your penis more toward her G-spot for enhanced stimulation. Also, angle your penis up and massage her middle wall. With your other hand, use the tips of your first and middle fingers to massage her clitoris, labia, and tang. [See Figure 5.32].

Another stimulation technique during doggy-style (not pictured) is to insert your thumb in her gem facing down and massage the top of your penis and around. Then reach down with your fingers to massage her clitoris while your penis is thrusting inside her vagina. Use your free hand to stimulate other areas (breasts, lips). Also, turn your thumb to face up and

Chapter Five

massage the upper walls.

Also, in doggy style position, insert your penis in her gem and use one hand to play with her clitoris and vagina. Turn your palm up and use your fingers to play with her clitoris and U-spot. Also, insert your thumb in her vagina to play with her G-spot.

Figure 5.32

Figure 5.33

Additionally, insert your fingers in her vagina to play with her perineal sponge while the other hand stimulates her gem area around your penis or her nipples [See Figure 5.33]. She can then reach in-between her legs to massage your balls as you slide in and out.

Also, position her on her knees doggy style in the middle of the bed; you can lay perpendicular behind her so you are forming a T. She positions her gem so it is facing down, and you slide into her gem. In this T position, you have a beautiful view of the profile of her body. Stimulate her breasts and neck with one hand while you grab, spank, massage, and jiggle her ass with the other hand. You can thrust hard, or she rides your penis in a sexy manner.

v. Naughty Butterfly

The Naughty Butterfly allows you to enjoy anal sex while you stimulate her clitoris and/or G-spot with vibration with no hands! Tadaaa! You'll be able to use your hands to stimulate other erogenous zones, and she can use her hands to arouse your erogenous zones. Since many women like anal sex with stimulation to their clitoris and G-spot, a butterfly toy that provides only simulation to her clitoris and vagina is a good solution (some also provide gem stimulation; don't get that version).

Butterfly toys come with straps so they stay secure on her clitoris. Your hands are free to massage around her gem, spank her ass, grab her waist, pull her hair, pleasure her breasts, and do the things that turn her on. She can use her hands to spread her ass cheeks, play with you, and support herself in a variety of positions. Your hands are free to support yourself in a variety of wild positions. Have her kneel on the bed with her ass close to her ankles; you lay perpendicular to her behind her and slide into her gem. Enjoy her gem while viewing her profile, seeing her bent over, and the curvatures of her body.

w. U-Spot Love

U-spot Love is similar to the V-Spot Vibe massage, but with some differences that your partner will enjoy. You'll be using a vibrating plug and focusing on her U-spot. Lick her clitoris and all around to start. Play with a vibrating plug around her gem while licking her. Insert the plug sensually until it is all the way inside, up to the stationary insertion point. Play with her perineal sponge by inserting both your ring finger and middle fingers into her vagina. Go deep inside to massage her A-spot [See Figure 3.12 from Chapter 3].

Chapter Five

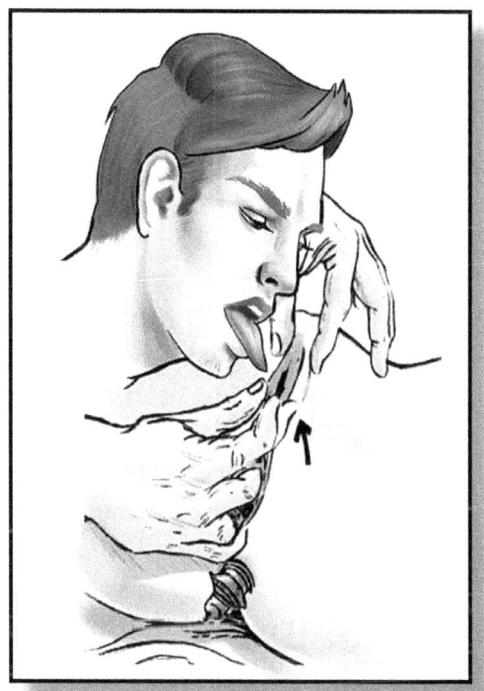

Figure 5.34

Use your thumb and first finger (same hand) to squeeze her lips sensually on the outside of her U-spot. Massage her U-spot from the sides; at the same time, your other hand's thumb and first finger are massaging her clitoris. Lick her simultaneously. Have her enjoy this for a bit. Now use the first finger from the hand that has the two fingers in her vagina to massage the U-spot directly.

Your finger will be below her clitoris but above or to the sides of her urinary hole. Massage the U-spot with small circles and apply a little bit of pressure. Flicker your finger side to side on the U-spot. Ask her what feels best. Get your feedback so you know what pressure she likes. Once you know, suck her clitoris with all your soul and with passionate energy. At the same time, stroke her clitoris with the other hand.

So all the following happens at the same time: sucking her clitoris, massaging her U-spot, G-spot, and perineal sponge all the while stimulating her gem with a vibrating plug! These are lots of simultaneous pleasures for her to enjoy [**See Figure 5.34**]!

x. *Bottoms Up*

Have her lay on her back and get in a 69 position or with her on her knees and ass in the air. Start by licking, sucking, and kissing her lips and clitoris. Add stimulation to her vagina with one hand and lube the middle finger of your other hand. Glide it over her gem. Lightly massage her gem ring in a circular motion, and at the same time, circle your tongue around her clitoris. Increase the pressure of your licking around her clitoris and simultaneously increase the pressure of your finger, massaging around her gem ring. Do so in a sensual manner.

Suck her clitoris into your lips; slide your finger around her gem ring to where it is in front of her tang. As you suck her clitoris passionately, press her gem ring towards her tang. Make your tongue stiffer and lick her U-spot. As you let her clitoris out of your lips, let off pressure from her gem and circle around her gem sensually. Do all of the above several times, synchronizing your licks and sucks with the movement of your finger to the beat of sensual/sex music. You are enabling her to enjoy the sensual experience with stimulation of multiple erogenous zones.

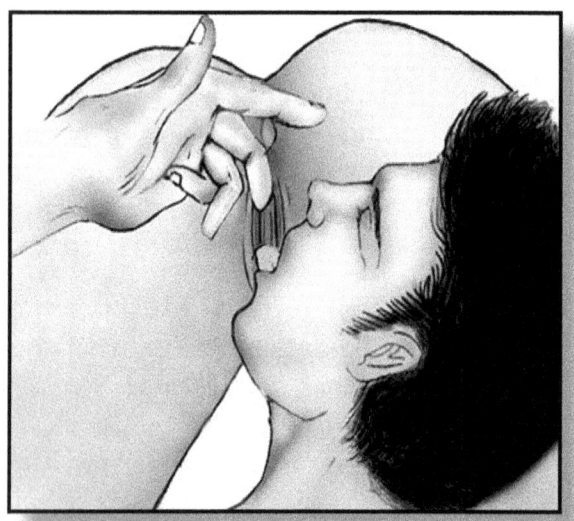

Figure 5.35

Now you are going to lick down to the bottom area of her vagina. Turn your head so that your lips are angled in the same direction as her lips. Take one side of her labia at the bottom of her vagina and sensually start sucking it into your mouth. Do this as if she is your favorite dessert. Suck her bottom labia deeply into your mouth, and go as deep as you can with your tongue into the bottom of her vagina. Send all your energy to your mouth. While you are doing this, use one to three fingers to play with and in her gem. Massage your tongue through her gem [**See Figure 5.35**].

Move your mouth to the bottom of her vagina; lick the bottom inner wall of her wetness as deeply and passionately as you can. Explore the bottom wall with your tongue. Moan and groan to provide vibration to the area. Now slowly move to the other side to suck her labia deeply into your mouth. As you finger her gem, sensually lick her tang and the edge of her

Chapter Five

gem ring. Since you are in a 69 position, she can be pleasuring you too, using both hands to pleasure you while she sucks.

y. Body Quake

Lay her on her side and place her butt at the edge of the bed. Use the Cordless Wand Massager on her clitoris and U-spot. Slide your penis into her vagina. Slide another vibrator into her gem. You can move the vibrator inside her gem in alternate movements opposite to your thrusting or in the same motion. The power of the Wand Massager will give her an earthshaking orgasm while you both enjoy anal sex [**See Figure 5.36**]!

You can switch it up, slide your penis into her gem, and use a new or thoroughly-washed vibrator in her vagina while the power massager is on her clitoris. She can also hold one or both toys while you use your hands and fingers to stimulate her in other erogenous zones. Also, try the **Double U Technique** that I covered in Chapter 4 under the dual motor toy for the Body Quake.

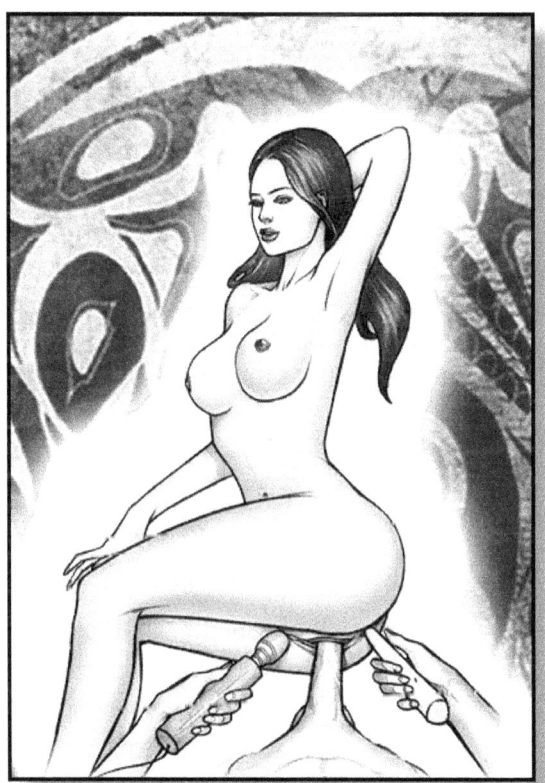

Figure 5.35

Use two dual-motor vibes to stimulate her clitoris, U-spot, G-spot, perineal sponge, and gem while you have sex with her. With the toys in place, use your hands to arouse other erogenous zones. If the toys need assistance to stay in place, she can keep the clitoris toy in place while you use one hand to keep the gem toy in place until she has an explosive orgasm! You'll enjoy the vibrations below and above your penis. Give her a remote control to change modes, and you can play with the other. You may also give both to her so she can go to town with vibration experimentation for both of you!

2. Hand Quake

Another variation of the Body Quake can be done without vibrators using your hands at the edge of the bed. Use the same position, or you can do this in a spooning position. Lubricate her everywhere and very well. Slide your penis into her vagina. Use one hand to play with her clitoris and U-spot with your palm and fingers and slide two fingers into her gem. Stroke your penis and fingers in and out at the same time, then alternate with your penis, going in as your fingers come out.

Do whatever you can with your mouth, lick her body, breasts, fingers, and engage in HOT sex talk. This can achieve an anal orgasm, a G-spot and vaginal orgasm, and a clitoral orgasm all at the same time! It is amazing to see, hear, and enjoy this beautiful event!

A second version of the Hand Quake after she is used to a lot of anal penetration is the My Vibe Technique but with wider vibrations/shaking of your penis going in and out of her vagina or gem. Grab the base of your penis while you are in her gem, move your penis up and down, and side to side fast and vigorously while you play with her clitoris. Adjust to the speed and shaking intensity that she likes best. Circle your penis around as well. The stronger and wider vibrations and shaking feels good because vibration has an arousing effect.

5.2 The Spice of Variety

There are many positions that you can do when having anal sex; the possibilities are immense. The key is that when you are introducing her to new positions, go slow at first to make sure it feels good for her. You want to make sure you are creating intimate and erotic moments. First, pleasure with anal play that she likes, then do a position you know she enjoys first before you try a new one. Use the vibrator on her clitoris to

Chapter Five

help aid a pleasurable entry, and massage her gem during anal sex so you are stimulating the area and keeping it well lubed at all times.

When introducing her to new positions, think about how you can stimulate all her senses, her clitoris, G-spot, U-spot, A-spot, gem, and her emotions. This will enable her to try to enjoy a variety of different positions and activities.

5.3 Tips to Maintain Enjoyment
Consistently enhance the experience

There are things your lover can do to help the process when you two are not together. How often you see each other will determine whether she might need to engage in gem play on her own. If you two have sex with each other two to three times a week, then she probably will not need to do her own gem play. However, if you see each other once a week or less, then too much time might be passing by between gem play opportunities to make consistent progress. Once you have taken her to the point of Night 3, when she is enjoying your finger, tongue, and plugs in her gem, then she can engage in masturbation with a finger, plug, or other toys to maintain the progress you two have made together.

Your partner can use the Berman Dilator set and other toys she likes. It's good practice to begin with a shower or bath and an anal flush. Then, she can set up the mood that turns her on, including lighting and music. The strategy here is for the woman to stimulate herself, and then play with a smaller plug at first and work up to bigger sizes. She can leave in a plug so that her gem gets used to the size while she plays with her vagina and clitoris. Women, remember to stimulate your clitoris as you put the toy or plug inside your gem.

Try masturbating while lying on your back or by bending over and reaching around. Depending on how comfortable she is with pictures and videos, you can have her make a video of herself masturbating with gem play, which would be a highly erotic turn on— mmm, mmm. You can watch it together and keep it on your phone. Chapter 8 of the book Anal Pleasure, and Health by Jack Morin, PhD, does a good job of explaining the biophysical response of anal masturbation scientifically. Also, Google "female anal masturbation." If there is hesitation, you'll find answers to many questions you may have. If you can have sex more frequently during the week with your lover, then do so as long as it feels good, but give yourself a little break if you are even slightly sore. Wait until you feel 100% ready. It is a very erotic experience for women to increase the size they can take inside their gem with their partner.

Some people are concerned that anal sex might stretch out or damage their anus. Feel comfort that millions of people have anal sex without this problem. Women's Health Magazine asked New York City sex therapist Ian Kerner, Ph.D., author of She Comes First, to weigh in. In his conclusion, Kerner states, If you're a fan of butt play, you don't have to give it up for fear of damaging that vital muscle, says Kerner. As it turns out, Kegels, the exercise made famous for strengthening your pelvic floor and possibly boosting your orgasm, can also tone up your sphincter. Kerner points out that he hasn't heard complaints about it from any of his clients who engage in anal sex.

While anal is relatively safe for your butt muscles, Kerner says there are a few other things you should be doing to keep your booty in healthy working order. He states to:

1. Use lube because the rectum does not lubricate, and lack of lubrication can lead to hemorrhoids.

2. Get loose; if you are tense, your sphincter will be too.

3. Use a condom since the anus contains lots of bacteria, and the man can get the bacteria in his urethra. The above three points are solved in the process and cleaning routine I propose.

4. Know your G.I. tract; if you suffer from Irritable Bowel Syndrome, do not pass go. Kerner says anal sex can trigger a bout of it, which is pretty much guaranteed to be a mood killer.

No matter what, keep this in mind: "If something feels wrong, it probably is wrong," says Kerner. "If you detect any irritation, it's time to give the butt a break."

The site WellandGood.com covered the topic and provided similar advice, the rectum is the last part of your large intestine, which leads to the anus, says Evan Goldstein MD, CEO and founder of Bespoke Surgical, a sexual-wellness company specializing in anal-related health.

Chapter Five

"There are actually three sets of muscles that comprise the anal sphincter, which is the last part of your anus." Two of these muscles are voluntarily controlled (relaxed and contracted), while the third operates involuntarily. For pleasurable and successful anal, all three of these need to be relaxed. How? Foreplay. The article continues to say, just as you can overstretch your hamstring in yoga, you can also overstretch your sphincter during anal if you push the boundaries of their anal elasticity. Your body will usually alert you via pain that what you're doing isn't A-okay.

Dr. Goldstein and Alicia Sinclair, certified sex educator, also feature in the article; both experts say the fear of damage shouldn't stop you from exploring butt play and pleasure with a partner you trust.

To tame your worries, practice preventative measures, like Kegels and pelvic-floor strengthening moves. Sinclair says yup, those famous do-anywhere vaginal-strengtheners also lend themselves to your anal sphincter. You might try strengthening them Hilaria Baldwin-style.

With a proper warm-up, lube, and exercises, you and your anal sphincter will be great! But if you do suffer any kind of injury, seek advice from a doc who specializes in sexual health.

As I stated at the end of Section 1.6, doing Kegels will provide a dual benefit of stronger orgasms and keeping your sphincter muscles healthy and strong. That said, I would not advise using gigantic plugs, toys, or objects that are considerably larger than the girth of your partner. I would recommend being cautious. If you want to use large items, do your research before, so you know how to do it safely.

In regards to proper preparation for her gem to stay healthy, that is the reason I instruct that every night after Night 1, you do the foreplay activities of all the nights previous to prepare for that evening. Even during the first several months after you have had anal sex for the first time, prepare her for your girth by using fingers and toys to gradually accustom her gem to take you in smoothly. Some women might need longer. Adjust accordingly based on how she feels.

For several weeks or more after you first had full anal penetration, less is more, don't pound hard and go for more than a half-hour in her gem. Slowly build up to stronger strokes and longer times based on how she feels during and after. Yes, her after gem sensation is just as important.

You want to ensure that even though she enjoyed the action during the sex session, that she does not end up with lots of soreness after. By gradually escalating the strength of your stroke and length of time across multiple sex sessions, her body will adapt in a comfortable manner. Give her gem a break of at least one day or two after a stronger session until she feels good during and after with the intensity of sex that you both like.

Anal sex and play is also a great way for women who have recently given birth to enjoy an erotic sexual experience while recovering from the birth process. Couples can have anal sex during the woman's menstrual cycle to continue to enjoy each other. Some people engage in anal sex to finish a sexual session and to reduce the chances of pregnancy, with the man orgasming in her gem. If you do this, do so on her back so that gravity pulls semen away from her vagina. As the semen comes out, wipe her with a cloth or baby wipe to make sure you further decrease the chances of cross-pollination. Not a 100% foolproof system, there is still a chance of pregnancy due to strong swimmers, but you can make your own assessment and system to minimize the chance of pregnancy.

5.4 Ever-Evolving Pleasure

This book was written with the woman in mind, to introduce her to a new high in sexual delight with anal play and anal sex. If you go through the process of pleasure laid out in this book, you'll have more than doubled the variety of things you can do sexually with more and stronger orgasms for her.

You must communicate together along the way and build trust by letting her know that if she feels any discomfort, slow down or stop, give her a rest, and try again later or at another time. Make sure she knows that, in this process, her pleasure and comfort are top priority, and any discomfort supersedes the desire to keep going. Kiss her passionately and make sure she does not feel that you are ever upset or frustrated. Let her know how much you appreciate her for exploring with you. Build intimacy to spark sexual exploration. Inspire her to yearn for more from the physical and emotional bliss. Anal sex will give her powerful orgasms in a variety of ways. Both of you will find many new methods, acts, and positions that will make you two explode. I wish couples incredible joy with their new found pleasure.

5.5 Erotic Flow Books

Read more about expressing your erotic soul and creating a variety of HOT sexual experiences that will keep thrilling your sex-life! Look for my book Sex On A New Level - The Art of Creating and Introducing New Sexual Experiences for a Lifetime of Exciting Sex. 2021 release. To pre-order email me at David@EroticFlow.com and I'll provide you 50% off the e-book.

As I mentioned in the Content Insights, reviews are the lifeblood for an author to make a difference and help others learn about the subject. YOUR HONEST REVIEW IS GREATLY APPRECIATED. Without it, the years of effort won't be able to help others.

1. Share the book with a friend.

2. Press the LIKE button on Amazon, it is anonymous.

3. When writing a review, even it is only one sentence or several words, that makes a huge difference in expanding awareness. If you would like to keep your privacy, reviews can be done with a different reviewer name.

4. View the Resources section for information on feedback.

Chapter Summary

Chapter Five ~ Erotic Anal Play ~
Delicious Stimulation for Both of You

5.1 Erotic AZ Play and Advanced Positions

The following summaries give a quick description of the type of sexual act involved in each activity.

a. The E3- Intercourse sex with simultaneous stimulation to the clitoris, vagina, and gem while in a cross position.

b. Palms of Pleasure - While inside her gem, you massage the area around her gem with one hand, lubricate her vagina area, insert your middle and ring finger into her vagina, and massage her clitoris.

c. The V-Spot Massage - This is a vagina-licking technique that pleasures the clitoris, the exterior and the interior of the vagina, and the gem.

d. The V-Spot Massage and Vibe Combo - This is a vagina-licking and vibrator technique that pleasures the clitoris, the exterior and interior vagina, and her gem.

e. Missionary Work - In a missionary position, while going inside of her gem, reach around with one or both hands, and massage the area around her gem, in between her vagina and her gem, and her clitoris. Also during vaginal missionary position, reach around to massage the same area, but also insert your finger, or fingers, inside her gem. Play around her vagina and tang.

Chapter Five

f. Tongue Tingle - Licking her gem, and massaging your tongue through the inside of her vagina.

g. Pleasure Twists - A gem-entry technique to help her enjoy the entry process.

h. The CrissCross - A clitoris-sucking and vagina pleasuring technique.

i. The Straddle and Flip - A vagina, gem-licking, and vibrator technique that delivers lots of excitement.

j. Good Vibes - An intercourse and gem sex technique with lots of vibrating stimulation for her and you.

k. Pearls - A gem-play and vagina-licking technique that adds pearls or silicone beads to accentuate pleasure.

l. Fingertips - A gem-, vagina-, and clitoris-play technique with which you will massage her inner walls for stimulation.

m. Eyes wide Shut - A fantasy technique to stimulate her whole body, arouse her senses, and thoroughly pleasure her gem.

n. Upside Down Gem Spot - An anal sex position that includes more pleasuring techniques than the typical porn scene.

o. Gem 69 - Exactly what it sounds like; it is how to enjoy licking her gem while she licks yours.

p. Upside down V-Lick - A deep gem-licking technique to put the warmth of your tongue into her beauty as deeply as possible. Also, a way to do the V-Spot Massage in the upside down position.

q. Ride-Em - Anal sex technique so she can have an anal and clitoral orgasm from riding you through pelvic stimulation.

r. Ride-Him On All Fours - An anal sex activity that enables both parties lots of freedom to thrust.

s. G&G - This activity stands for gem and G-spot. This position will give her G-spot stimulation while you are in her gem with your penis.

t. Reverse Cowgirl Massage - A hot position where the girl straddles you, looking away from you. Add the finger techniques provided for stimulation to greatly enhance her excitement.

u. Bend Over Beautiful - Another way to pleasure her is to have her in doggy style position; go into her vagina with your penis (remember, wash thoroughly if it is after anal sex, or switch rubbers). Insert a finger or two in her gem while you massage her clitoris with other fingers.

v. Naughty Butterfly - A butterfly toy, a good solution for hands-free stimulation of her clitoris, while you do a variety of positions. You can now massage around her gem, spank her ass, grab her waist, pull her hair, pleasure her breasts, and do the things that turn her on.

w. U-spot Love - Insert a Vibrating Plug until it is all the way into the stationary position. Play with her perineal sponge. Use your thumb and first finger to squeeze her lips sensually on the outside of her U-spot. Massage her U-spot directly.

x. Bottoms Up - Lick to the bottom area of her vagina. Suck her bottom labia deeply, and then lick the bottom of her vagina deeply.

y. Body Quake - With her ass at the edge of the bed, use a powerful wand type massager on her clitoris. Insert your penis in her vagina, and another vibrator in her gem. Another option to try with clean toys is to insert your penis in her gem and a vibrator in her vagina while the power massager is on her clitoris. You can also use the Lelo Sona Cruise 2 instead of the wand. Do the Double U technique. Use two dual motor vibrators, one for her clitoris and G-spot and another for her perineal sponge and gem while you have vaginal sex.

z. Hand Quake - Variation of the Body Quake can be done without the vibrators, and you can use your hands. Use the MyVibe Technique with stronger/wider movement.

Chapter Five

5.2 The Spice of Variety

To introduce her to a variety of anal sex positions, make sure you are always stimulating all her senses, and multiple erogenous zones: her clitoris, G-spot, U-spot, A-spot, Cul-de-sac, labia and gem, but most of all her mind, body (all over), and soul.

5.3 Tips to Maintain Enjoyment

If you only have sex with your partner once a week or less, you will need her to practice her own anal play in-between your together sessions. This is important so she does not lose the progress made during those sessions. If she plays at the girth where you left off at least once, preferably twice a week, she will maintain the progress you made during your sessions together.

5.4 Ever-Evolving Pleasure

You have now more than doubled your sexual knowledge and the variety of positions available to you. Just to recap the pleasure process: seduce her body and mind simultaneously throughout the process. If you ever proceed at a pace that is not comfortable for her, stop and let her adjust, and only do what is pleasurable for her. Do this so well until she is yearning for more. Let her know her comfort is top priority. Anal sex will give her powerful orgasms in a variety of ways. Both of you will find many new methods, acts, and positions that will make you two explode. I wish couples incredible joy with their new found pleasure.

5.5 Erotic Flow Books

This is a sensual, intimate, passionate, fun, and erotic journey. Email me at David@EroticFlow.com for a 50% discount on my next book and Sex On A New Level - The Art of Creating and Introducing New Sexual Experiences for a Lifetime of Exciting Sex. 2021 release.

Author Bio

Continuation from the Content Insights Section. The second reason I wrote this book because creating new sexual experiences is a core passion of mine. My story starts many moons ago. Ever since I was very young, I have been highly interested in sex. When others played with GI Joe, I was trying to kiss the girl I had a crush on. I was just a child and had to be creative to come up with games and activities.

Another aspect of my life that has empowered my ability to innovate is that I have had to solve various health problems, from heart problems and surgeries since I was eight years old to broken bones, wound infections, and joint dislocations. I was a bit of an adventurer/daredevil in my younger days. But I've grown out of my rambling ways (quote from the Black Keys - I Got Mine). Necessity is definitely the mother of invention. I have had lots of necessities, and therefore, I have had to develop strong invention skills.

Throughout my life, I have applied creativity to many endeavors and especially sexuality. I LOVE to create sexual experiences, design fantasies, and pleasure the woman in my heart. Designing new experiences typically starts at Home Depot! A construction supply store for those outside of the U.S. I walk in, and the reps say, DeCitore is here! Yes, it's him, and he's got a big ole grin on his face! You know he's not fixing a bathroom or kitchen sink! He's on the move! Follow him; he's headed to the ceiling hooks, ropes, and tie-downs! Kidding aside, I do go to Home Depot or Lowes to create fantasies, and once the set-up is done, you can hide and re-use.

In my twenties, I read dozens of books on sex, and when the Internet came about, I conducted lots of online research. I attained undergrad education and in my thirties, I completed a masters; therefore, my research skills have been well-honed, and I continued my research on sexuality.

In my late thirties, a girlfriend stated that I should write a book to help couples that are new to anal sex have a good experience. Before our relationship, she had a bad experience and thought she never wanted to try again. However, she enjoyed the process I had developed, and thereupon loved anal sex from the pleasure and powerful orgasms that she had. She thought other couples would benefit from the process. Writing the content became a passion project to help couples and women have a good experience with anal stimulation and sex, and not the typical bad one.

That kicked my research into turbo to see if there was a good solution already in the market. From my MBA training, I did a thorough competitive analysis of the market to ensure my content had differentiated value. It turned out there were many books and resources on the market, but only two books were top sellers. Although, neither of them or the other books and resources I found covered the introduction phase well. Thus, why women still had bad experiences.

I bought many books and DVDs, watched online videos, read lots of articles, and attended sex conferences to see what in-person classes had to offer. It turned out that I did have a differentiated solution. Therefore, I launched the book in December of 2010. To my surprise and delight, it started climbing in sales by February, and by mid-March, it was the number one selling book on the subject of anal sex in the U.S. It reached a rank of #3 in the Psychology of Sexuality out of all sex books. It climbed to an Amazon sales rank in the low 4,000s and was the #1 selling book on anal sex on Amazon every day until April of 2012.

Then, Amazon type-casted all authors on the topic of anal sex as "adult." Books on the topic would no longer be found in an All Departments search or be promoted in the Customers Also Bought recommendation engine. That ruined sales for all of the authors on the topic. The book made over $200,000 in revenues within two years, and I received nice feedback from a range of young to older couples across 12 countries. A couple in their sixties from Canada wrote me a thankful review. I received similar reviews from Brazil, Japan, and India. Older couples appreciated a caring solution to spice up their love life. With the advent of Viagra, couples are having sex well into their later years.

After a decade, I updated the book with an even better system (explained in Content Insights). Moreover, I wrote a new book called Sex On A New Level - The Art of Creating and Introducing New Sexual Experiences for a Lifetime of Exciting sex. © 2020 Release in 2021. It has been a passion project to share content on detailed techniques and erotic sex experiences to increase excitement in short or long-term relationships. With over 30 years of creating various sexual fantasies and stimulation techniques, I am confident I can share information that will help some couples and hope I will make a positive difference in inspiring a passion for conceiving creative sexual experiences.

Resources

Webpage with Links

EroticFlow.com/HUP - Private page for paperback customers. If you navigate to EroticFlow.com, enter the URL again to get back. Check the site for updates to content. If you have site questions, contact me at David@EroticFlow.com.

Books

Emily Nagoski, Ph.D., Come As You Are: The Surprising New Science that Will Transform Your Sex Life © 2015

Ian Kerner, She Comes First: The Thinking Man's Guide to Pleasuring a Woman © 2009

Paul Joannides Psy. D, Guide to Getting it On: Unzipped © 2017

Charley Ferrer, Sex Unlimited: The ultimate secrets to dating and erotic pleasures © 2012

Alan P. Braur M.D. and Donna J. Brauer The New Promise of Pleasure for Couples ESO: How you and your lover can give each other hours of Extended Sexual Orgasm © 1983

Cathy Winks and Anne Semans, The Good Vibrations Guide to Sex © 2002

Don Miguel Ruiz, The Mastery of Love: A practical guide to the art of relationship © 1999

Dudley Seth Danoff, M.D., F.A.C.S., Superpotency: How to get it, use it, and maintain it for a lifetime © 1993

Eric Fromm, The Art of Loving © 1956

Eve Eschner Hogan, M.A. with Steve Hogan, Intellectual Foreplay: Questions for Lovers & Lovers-to-be © 2000

Graham Masterton, How to Drive Your Woman Wild in Bed © 1987

Jack Morin, Ph.D., Anal Pleasure and Health: A guide for men and women 3rd edition, © 2008

Jack Morin, The Erotic Mind: Unlocking the inner sources of sexual passion and fulfillment © 1995

Kerry and Diane Riley, Tantric Secrets for Men: What every woman will want her man to know about enhancing sexual ecstasy © 2002

Lonnie Garfield Barbach PH.D., For Yourself: The fulfillment of female sexuality © 1975

Mantak and Maneewan Chia, Douglas Abrams and Rachel Carlton Abrams-M.D., The Multi-Orgasmic Couple: How couples can dramatically enhance their pleasure, intimacy, and health © 2000

Michael Morgenstern, How to Make Love to a Woman © 1982

Nina Hartley with I.S. Levine, Nina Hartley's Guide to Total Sex © 2006

Susan and Clyde Hendrick, Liking, Loving, and Relating © 1991

Female with Female Toys

Ladies, you can do everything as instructed; all you need to do during Night Six and Seven is to use a strap-on holster with a vibrating dildo. You can start with a small vibrating dildo and work your way up to bigger sizes if desired. You can also perform the activities in Chapter Five. Here is an option for the holster, **Strap-on Harness Adjustable Universal Adult Sex Toy with 3 Different Sized O-Rings Suction Cup Dildo Compatible Harness** , or this holster with multi-penetration for the woman wearing the harness, **The Strap-on Dildo 3 Removable Silicone Dildos with Harness**.

For vibrating dildos, you can start with a five-inch dildo like this one, **California Exotics Shower Stud Super Stud.** Then, add a bigger size. Here is a seven inch option, **7" Vibrating Heated Dildo with Remote**

Resources

Control. Go even bigger if you like, this one is 8.6 inches, heats up, swings, and thrusts, **Realistic Dildo Telescopic Heating Vibrating Dildo, Powerful Swinging Thrusting Dildo**. With all of the options available to you online, you both will enjoy amazing orgasms!

Do-It-Yourself

You can do the process by yourself; all you need is the toys to replicate the licking, sucking, and Grooves For Her technique. Here is a toy option for licking, **The Tongue Vibrator with Clit Tickler for G-spot & Clitoral Stimulation**, and here is a toy for licking and sucking, **The Licking Clitoris Sucker Toy.** To replicate the non-penetrative knuckle sensations of the Grooves For Her technique, use this toy, **Doc Johnson Classic - The Fist**; it resembles the appropriate hand shape better. Along with the toys you want to use from Chapter Four, you can enjoy amazing anal orgasms on your own.

Additional Anal Sexuality Resources

Beducated.com, an online magazine dedicated to sex education, released an article titled "**Anal Orgasm—the Back Door to Heaven**." The author of the article, Mariah Freya, founder of Beducated and sex and orgasm coach, states not only that anal orgasms are real but also that she herself enjoys them. She says, "Today, when the urge and desire for anal sex arises, I turn into an animal. I now set aside my ego and let the wild side in me rule the show. I moan deeper, I move stronger, and I breathe like a bull. The anal orgasm sensation is like sensual steam that rises to the roof. It is a clap of thunder that comes from deep below and ascends. An anal orgasm is earth-shaking, profound, and exquisite."

Yahoo's Lifestyle section also issued an article in July 2015 called "**The 12 Types of Orgasms—What They Are & How to Have Them**." The article states that for many women, anal intercourse feels fantastic.

Web Resources

The **EroticFlow.com** website is getting revamped. Currently, you will find services to enhance the learning experience such as a group webinar or online consulting covered below. The website will have erotic art, new toys, events, and more resources on overall sex. Customers on the mailing list know will get notified when it is done. Send an email to **List@EroticFlow.com**. If you request to that get on the list, I will send you a pleasuring technique and a fantasy set-up and execution from the new book. Also visit YouTube.com/EroticFlow for curated videos on sex instruction from other educators.

Music

Many times couples do not have the time to select the best music to set the mood for a hot and passionate encounter with their lover. It takes time to look for the best music, to sequence it right, to set up music that will deliver a specific vibe that you want, so you two can flow together just right. Whether you want the vibe to be sensual, passionate, romantic, erotic, or a combination, it takes a lot of time to have a large collection to keep things new and exciting. I have done the work for you! I have been collecting music to enhance the experience of flow since 1992. To have different sexual vibes and without having to invest the time to collect and sequence a large selection songs, I compiled music playlists for you at **YouTube.com/EroticFlow.**

Consulting

For couples that want education or fantasy creation for a special night or to address the needs of a specific situation, Erotic Flow Consulting is the solution. Learn more about Erotic Flow Consulting on the About page of the website.

Webinars

For people who live far away and who would like to learn through a webinar format, I present the content with Q&A session so that a group of people can get specific questions answered. As well as learn from the questions of others for a lower price than private consulting.

Erotic Terminology

This book is designed to arouse the mind of a woman. I had originally wrote the book with erotic terminology but changed it to clinical terminology to meet guidelines to reach a broader audience. Though the terms are clinical, I invite you to fantasize the wording, scenery, music, smells, tastes, and erotic feelings that turn you on the most to bring the explanations to life in your mind.

Anal Sex Health Research

http://en.wikipedia.org/wiki/anal_sex

http://www.netdoctor.co.uk/sexandrelationships/analsex.htm

http://en.wikipedia.org/wiki/Anal_canal

http://www.scribd.com/doc/86887/10-Rules-of-Anal-Sex-by-Jack-Morin

http://en.wikipedia.org/wiki/Anal_masturbation

Feedback is Crucial and Rewarded

VERY IMPORTANT: Thank you for taking the time to read this book. The only way to improve the book and help other couples and, most importantly, women have a good experience with anal sex is to share your feedback. The ideas and experiences of others are extremely valuable and can provide knowledge that can help many. Authors pour their heart and soul into writing their books. if you have suggestions. requests, or questions, I gladly welcome them. Please email me and share your thoughts at **David@EroticFlow.com**. As a token of my appreciation, I will reward you by sending you a pleasuring technique and fantasy to perform with setup, execution, and positions from my new book.

Your feedback and reviews will help women not go through a bad experience and enable them to enjoy a very pleasurable, sensual, and intimate experience. What feedback to provide:

1. Did the book provide the content/solution you were looking for?

2. What you liked?

3. What needs changing (delete, less, more, or different on anything)?

4. What helped you most (sharing your story can make a huge difference)?

Share to Help

If this book provided a better experience in exploring anal sexuality, if you enjoyed some of the pleasuring techniques, or if you learned something that you think could also benefit others, then share the book with friends. There are so many people that do not know of the new scientific research that shows women that engage in anal play and sex have more and stronger orgasms.

Let others know about the book by tweeting that you finished the book, liking the Facebook.com/EroticFlow page. If you do not want to share with your friends that you read the book, just tell them that you read an article online about it in case the topic of anal sex comes up. **On the Amazon page or other online shops, writing a review, indicating which reviews are helpful, or clicking the LIKE button, is extremely helpful (all can be done anonymously).** If you have the ability to tell a lot of people and want to make good money by receiving a percentage of every sale, read about the Partner Marketing program on the About EF page at EroticFlow.com.

Flowing is Giving

I wish you the best in your journey of passion, intimacy, and erotic ecstasy. Erotic Flow was created to help others. A portion of the proceeds from this book will go to help people in a variety of worthwhile charities in areas such as health, community development, and preservation of the environment. Read more about our giving efforts at the About EF section on the EF site. Live it to the fullest!

Spice Up Your Tech

Background resources from SkinIt.com and DecalSkin.com Visit SkinIt.com and DecalSkin.com to personalize your technology. Go through the EF site for discounts to the above sites.

Community

Thank you to all the people who read this book. I hope to continue to build a relationship with you and together we can make this world a better place. The community we build will inspire people to create incredible life experiences, contribute to people in need, and help the environment.

Disclaimer

The information contained herein is for private informational purposes. Any facts are as timely as possible but things change. The publisher, author, editors, distributors, or booksellers do not endorse, condone, authorize, confirm, or sanction anal sexuality in regions of the country where the practice is illegal and are not responsible for health issues resulting from unsafe experimentation. Military couples should refer to the Uniform Code of Military Justice, Art. 125, for restrictions on sexual practices.

Enjoy Erotic Music Playlists and EF's Favorite YouTube videos on Dating, Relationships, Sex, and More at YouTube.com/EroticFlow.

Get Social at

Facebook.com/EroticFlow, We Love Your Likes.

Learn Erotic Facts and History at Twitter.com/EroticFlow.

Let's Be Friends and meet more friends at Facebook.com/DavidDeCitore.

www.ingramcontent.com/pod-product-compliance
Lightning Source LLC
Chambersburg PA
CBHW071703090426
42738CB00009B/1643